"This book is a treasure for any teen wanting to work more effectively with their ADHD. Using simple, easy-to-do, yet incredibly powerful exercises, young people will be able to use the resources of mindfulness and self-compassion to be calmer and more focused in daily life."

—**Kristin Neff, PhD**, associate prof
The University of Texas at Austin

"Mindfulness and self-compassion are a powerful formula for a happy and successful life. This book shows you easy ways to steady your mind, follow through on what you want to do, and quiet the critical voices in your head. It's written by experts who know their stuff, but it's best to trust your *own* experience. Give mindfulness and self-compassion a try, and see what happens."

—**Christopher Germer, PhD**, part-time lecturer in
the department of psychiatry at Harvard Medical School,
and coauthor of *The Mindful Self-Compassion Workbook*

"This is a gentle and effective workbook packed with important and practical information for teens with ADHD. Bertin and Bluth capture the most essential ingredients in leading a successful life with ADHD: acceptance and self-compassion. This book achieves an alchemy of scientific-driven information and friendly accessibility so that teens can approach this guide with openness, in the effort of being their most authentic and optimal selves."

—**Roberto Olivardia, PhD**, clinical psychologist and
lecturer in the department of psychiatry at Harvard
Medical School

"Bertin and Bluth make mindfulness accessible, interesting, and even fun in their book, *Mindfulness and Self-Compassion for Teen ADHD*. It is written in a style that teens with ADHD can read thoroughly. The combination of Bertin and Bluth's specializations make for an engaging book that covers the spectrum of teen experiences with ADHD. Their book is recommended for teens with ADHD, those that want to learn more about mindfulness, and clinicians who will appreciate this effective workbook."

—**Stephanie Moulton Sarkis, PhD**, psychotherapist and
author of *Gaslighting* (http://www.stephaniesarkis.com)

"This great book shares a bunch of good strategies for staying on top of the practical matters of ADHD, but more importantly, it will help you to live a happier life where you get to call more of the shots. Some of those frustrating ADHD challenges will remain, but a mindful approach will help you keep your head on and bring your best to those challenges."

—**Ari Tuckman, PsyD**, author, international speaker,
and ADHD expert

the *i*nstant help
solutions series

Young people today need mental health resources more than ever. That's why New Harbinger created the **Instant Help Solutions Series** especially for teens. Written by leading psychologists, physicians, and professionals, these evidence-based self-help books offer practical tips and strategies for dealing with a variety of mental health issues and life challenges teens face, such as depression, anxiety, bullying, eating disorders, trauma, and self-esteem problems.

Studies have shown that young people who learn healthy coping skills early on are better able to navigate problems later in life. Engaging and easy-to-use, these books provide teens with the tools they need to thrive—at home, at school, and on into adulthood.

This series is part of the **New Harbinger Instant Help Books** imprint, founded by renowned child psychologist Lawrence Shapiro. For a complete list of books in this series, visit newharbinger.com.

mindfulness & self-compassion for **teen adhd**

build executive functioning skills, increase motivation & improve self-confidence

MARK BERTIN, MD
KAREN BLUTH, PhD

Instant Help Books
An Imprint of New Harbinger Publications, Inc.

Publisher's Note

INSTANT HELP, the Clock Logo, and NEW HARBINGER are trademarks of New Harbinger Publications, Inc.

Distributed in Canada by Raincoast Books

Copyright © 2021 by Mark Bertin and Karen Bluth
Instant Help Books
An imprint of New Harbinger Publications, Inc.
5674 Shattuck Avenue
Oakland, CA 94609
www.newharbinger.com

Cover design by Amy Shoup; Illustrations by Elizabeth McGoldrick

Acquired by Tesilya Hanauer; Edited by Karen Schader

Library of Congress Cataloging-in-Publication Data

Names: Bertin, Mark, (Psychologist) author. | Bluth, Karen, author.
Title: Mindfulness and self-compassion for teen ADHD : build executive functioning skills, increase motivation, and improve self-confidence / Mark Bertin and Karen Bluth.
Description: Oakland : New Harbinger Publications, 2021. | Series: Instant help solutions | Includes bibliographical references.
Identifiers: LCCN 2020048473 (print) | LCCN 2020048474 (ebook) | ISBN 9781684036394 (trade paperback) | ISBN 9781684036400 (pdf) | ISBN 9781684036417 (epub)
Subjects: LCSH: Self--Juvenile literature. | Compassion--Juvenile literature. | Mindfulness (Psychology)--Juvenile literature. | Attention-deficit hyperactivity disorder--Juvenile literature.
Classification: LCC BF697 .B4634 2021 (print) | LCC BF697 (ebook) | DDC 155.20835--dc23
LC record available at https://lccn.loc.gov/2020048473
LC ebook record available at https://lccn.loc.gov/2020048474

Printed in the United States of America

23   22   21

10   9   8   7   6   5   4   3   2   1   First Printing

Contents

Foreword

It is with great pleasure that I welcome you to this helpful, sensitive, and thoughtful book about teens with ADHD written for teens with ADHD. Not only is ADHD in teens vastly understudied in research, but there are few trade books written on the topic. And most of those are written for parents of teens with ADHD, not for the teens directly. Yet the teens with ADHD with whom I have worked, and who have come to accept that they have this condition, often hunger for advice on how to cope with and succeed with it—advice that's written just for them and with their point of view in mind. This book strives to do just that; it provides direct assistance in easily understandable prose that may just change your life for the better.

Teens with ADHD struggle with a disorder that involves far more than just inattention or feeling restless or talking a lot. Underneath those surface problems are more serious ones that relate to self-regulation. For people to develop self-regulation and employ it effectively, they must develop their executive functions—that set of mind tools that arise mainly from the prefrontal areas of the brain and the connections these areas have to other brain systems that they must govern. The executive networks of the brain are crucial for developing self-control, time management, planning and problem-solving, the skill of choosing appropriate goals and then attaining them, managing emotions, and self-motivation to support one's goals and welfare. In short, self-regulation is about anticipating and directing your behavior toward the impending future so that you can have a better future, and not just behave in ways aimed at the moment or now. The development of these mind tools of executive function is what ADHD disrupts. And it does so through no fault of your own—ADHD is among the most genetically influenced and brain-based disorders known to mental health professionals. Yet even though you did not ask to have this disorder, or do anything wrong in developing it, it is ultimately your responsibility to deal with it.

That is because teens with untreated ADHD are not just prone to doing poorly at school and having more conflicts with their parents at home, they are also more likely to engage in risk-taking in many domains of life—impulsive behavior that can end badly, result in more risk for accidental injuries, and make them more than twice as likely to die from that risk-taking than is the case with typical teens. That risk-taking can also cause major problems for them when they are trying to become more independent of their parents, have more of a say in their life's activities, make and keep new friends, and develop closer more intimate relationships with others. Having poor self-control can also create major problems for teens when they engage in driving a motor vehicle, learn about sex and engage in sexual relations with others, participate in sports without getting seriously injured, wisely manage the money they may start to earn through part or full time employment, and try to steer clear of the many opportunities they will encounter to experiment with unhealthy or illegal substances. This book is about how to cope with, make accommodations for, improve, and succeed with ADHD and its executive function deficits so that you can have a far better quality of life. Reading it may not only improve your life; it could just wind up saving it. That is why I am so glad you chose to open this cover and read this book. It is the first brick in building the path to the better life you know you deserve and can attain.

—Russell A. Barkley, PhD
    Clinical Professor of Psychiatry, Virginia Commonwealth
      University Medical Center
    Richmond, Virginia

CHAPTER 1

What Is ADHD Anyway?

You want to be independent and happy. You want to have fun, less stress, success, and good friends, and to choose a road into your own independent future. It's what most teens want.

If you are reading this book, something is likely getting in the way.

You may know exactly what you want to accomplish. But it seems way too hard. You are not quite getting there—yet.

Maybe a classmate has teased you about having ADHD. (By the way, when we say "ADHD," it includes what gets called ADD.) Maybe you've wondered if you have ADHD, or a doctor has diagnosed you.

Most importantly, what does ADHD even mean? And why does someone who cares about you say you have it?

People often talk about ADHD like it's only about attention. But it's really more about keeping up with goals. ADHD makes sticking to plans hard, like studying or exercising regularly.

I didn't realize until college that ADHD was the reason I was always stressed and running late, and forgot things.

—John, age 20

As ADHD expert Dr. Russell Barkley describes it, ADHD is not a disorder of not knowing what to *do*, it is a disorder of not doing what you *know*. People with ADHD know what should happen but have a hard time getting it done. That experience often affects their self-confidence and how they feel about themselves.

For example, you probably want to do well in school—though that may not feel possible right now. It feels hard keeping up with your assignments and responsibilities, because remembering, planning, and focusing are all part of ADHD. Or maybe your ADHD causes you to behave in ways your friends and family find off-putting, often without your realizing what's happened until afterward. Maybe you want to thrive in sports or a favorite hobby but haven't yet—because you rarely remember to practice. As you might now guess, that's all part of ADHD too.

Sometimes, you may feel completely alone in struggling this way, like no one else has traveled this road. The things you struggle with seem to come to others so easily. But the reality is, ADHD doesn't make you different, even if it feels that way. ADHD makes you more the *same* as everyone—dealing with your challenges, as others have theirs.

One way to reframe ADHD is this: Nearly everyone has a health issue, like asthma or diabetes or needing glasses. ADHD *is* a medical condition—one that affects focus, behavior, and planning. It's also very common. Roughly one out of twenty children and teens throughout the world has it.[1] In fact, the most common reason someone has ADHD is that it runs in families. So, if you have ADHD, you are most certainly not alone!

In this chapter, we'll look at what ADHD is, how it affects your life, and how various tools that support the growth of mindfulness, self-compassion, and executive function (you'll see what that is soon) can help.

What ADHD Is

How did someone decide you have ADHD? ADHD isn't like strep throat; there's no definitive test to diagnose it.

The only way to figure out if someone has ADHD is proving that certain traits both persist and cause that person a significant problem. Everyone matures at their own pace. But ongoing difficulties with managing day-to-day life, at school or at home, or even around our health, emotions, or relationships, might be caused by ADHD.

Some people with ADHD struggle most with inattention. This leads to challenges like having a hard time focusing on difficult activities (sometimes even ones they enjoy), daydreaming, or being overly disorganized. Others have more external signs like fidgeting or impulsiveness. Most people experience some of both. Plus, everyone's ADHD changes in different situations and as they age.

In general, ADHD makes juggling your responsibilities harder. It gets in the way of remembering details and keeping track of time, and makes it far too easy to procrastinate. Memorizing that vocabulary list? *I'll get to it on the bus*, you think. But on the bus, something else comes up, and you forget.

Sometimes I get down on myself. No one else I know seems to have to work as hard to get things done. I always manage, but it's so hard sometimes keeping up.

—Blake, age 16

Most importantly, having ADHD means your challenges impact your life significantly. Everyone gets distracted sometimes. Most people act impulsively occasionally. Lots of people fall short of their goals. Someone with ADHD experiences those symptoms as an ongoing strug-gle—feeling anxious, never getting the grades they want, or maybe even always overeating despite knowing better.

Whatever people say about you and your ADHD, remember this: having ADHD does not mean someone is "good" or "bad." It's about figuring out how ADHD affects *you* and doing something about it. ADHD may impact you at school, or with friends or family. It can play out as stress or forgetfulness or problems managing time—like spending too much time playing video games. It's not a judgment of you—it only means you have a tough time with specific life skills you'll want to work on.

To be absolutely clear: ADHD has nothing to do with your intelli-gence or motivation. Unfortunately, other people can make you feel that way: *un*intelligent or *un*motivated. You may feel that everyone around you always tells you what to do. "Stop playing and do your homework." "Stop giving your sister such a hard time." "Don't eat that, eat this."

Realistically, that feedback can be useful. Annoying maybe, but a reminder that makes it easier for you to stay on task. But if you feel others *constantly* correct you, it starts to affect how you feel about yourself.

ADHD can make you seem, or feel, lazy, disrespectful, or not great at school. It may look like you're not getting anywhere, which comes across like you're not trying. Or perhaps your parents, teachers, coaches, and every other adult under the sun make you feel like you aren't trying hard *enough*. And that hurts, because you are always trying to do your best. Sometimes you may begin to believe them and lose confidence in yourself.

Noticing that tendency to be overly harsh with ourselves (*I always screw up when it matters!*) is a first step to handling ADHD. When we feel down on ourselves, it's hard to stay strong and persistent. *I'll never be what they want me to be.* After all, how can you manage your ADHD if you don't believe you're capable?

Right now, it's like ADHD drives your car for you. It leads you off-task, and then even further off-road when your confidence erodes. With the right tools—ones this book will teach you—you will feel comfortable showing yourself and the world your true self. Accommodations can help you learn how to plan and organize and work *with* your brain. You can confidently put yourself in the driver's seat: making choices that get you where you need, all on your own—no reminders required.

Keeping Your Eyes on the Road

You're busy and maybe overwhelmed by life and school. Possibly the last thing you want is to read another book. But to take back the wheel from all the adults managing your life right now, or from your ADHD, give this book a try.

This book teaches you skills to overcome your ADHD. That starts with two called mindfulness and self-compassion. *Mindfulness* is the ability to be aware of what's going on when it's happening. It helps you slow down, even in times of stress, and figure out how to best handle a particular situation.

Self-compassion is being kind to yourself when you're having a hard time—treating yourself the same way you would a good friend. It helps quiet the critical inner voice that comes up when you make a mistake or struggle to do something you know you should. That critical voice is human—we all have it—but it gets in your way if you listen to it too much and let it overwhelm you. We'll be talking more about that later.

Each chapter includes both mindfulness and self-compassion practices that introduce skills you can use in your day-to-day life. Some are more formal, putting aside a few minutes each day for mindfulness or self-compassion practice. Others are more informal and used in real time when you feel angry, stressed, or frustrated. They'll help you slow down and figure out your best and most caring course of action.

We'll dive into these practices now, first looking at how mindfulness makes living with ADHD easier.

How Can Mindfulness Help?

With or without ADHD, we spend a lot of time tuned out from what's actually happening. We are here physically, but our minds are off somewhere else, and we react out of habit to whatever happens. We don't give our moment-to-moment choices much attention at all. This is when situations can escalate.

For example, your sister says, "You lost your homework again?! You're a mess!" You immediately respond, "I'm rubber, you're glue. Whatever you say bounces off me and sticks to you!" It's a little-kid comeback, but it's the first thing that comes to mind. You feel disrespected, and she's annoying. Of course, that comment triggers her to counter back, which angers you more. A back-and-forth exchange builds into a full-fledged fight.

What makes the ordeal especially frustrating is that your ADHD makes you react without first thinking the situation through. You don't even realize what you're doing and then have to deal with what happened. Maybe you think, *What's wrong with me? I can't do a single thing right.* The situation spirals out of control, and you feel bad afterward.

But in reality, you *can* help yourself stay ahead of your own reactions in these situations. Mindfulness allows for just that. Mindfulness doesn't mean acting any particular way. It means staying aware of what's going on without judging yourself.

When you're aware of what's happening in this nonjudgmental way, you see what's up in your life more clearly. Seeing our lives accurately, we are more purposeful about what to do (or not do). Maybe you see that your sister judged you in a way that stings. Maybe you take a breath and settle first, rather than lashing out. You can stay silent, if that makes sense, or let her know how her comment made you feel, so she understands it was hurtful.

When we learn to notice our reactions and catch ourselves, that creates an opportunity: We can choose what to say. We have the chance to tone down a tense situation instead of adding to it. We could even decide to make the *same* joke as always because it's funny and we know it won't be taken wrong. That's important too. We still get to be ourselves when we practice mindfulness.

The mindfulness skills introduced in this book help you stay aware of your thoughts and emotions, which lets you manage them more easily. One of the most effective ways of doing this starts with bringing attention to physical sensations in our body. That may seem weird, but it is pretty simple. Our mind wanders somewhere else. Our body can't be anywhere but here. That's all.

We're going to work with that idea in our first mindfulness practice, often called Soles of the Feet.[2] You can download an audio recording of this practice at https://www.newharbinger.com/46394.

INFORMAL PRACTICE: **Soles of the Feet**

Wherever you are, stand up. Start to notice the feeling of your feet on the floor.

As best as you're able, pay attention to the sensations on the bottom of your feet. Does the floor feel warm or cool? Soft or hard? Do you feel any tightness of your socks or shoes?

Don't try to make anything happen. Only notice what is here. Is there any sense of comfort or discomfort on the bottoms of your feet?

You will notice at some point your attention wanders. When that happens, simply direct your attention back to the soles of your feet.

If you like, try shifting your weight a bit. First to one foot, then to the other.

When you do this, what do you notice on the bottoms of your feet? Does anything change?

Any time your mind wanders, gently—without judging yourself—bring your attention back to the bottoms of your feet.

You're not trying to make anything happen in particular, simply noticing sensations that are already there.

Continue doing this for about five minutes.

You just did your first mindfulness practice! That's how mindfulness starts…with nothing more than noticing the physical sensations you're feeling. When we're noticing physical sensations, we know we aren't lost in thought. We're off autopilot and fully aware of what's going on.

As you can see, mindfulness practices like this are easy to understand. The hard part is remembering to do them. It's even harder to stay aware during our days with a million things going on. But don't worry. We'll be giving you lots of opportunity to learn and build these skills.

Mindfulness is like rehearsing scales on the piano or practicing free throws at the basket. When you repeat a skill enough, it shows up naturally in your life, whether in a big game, a piano recital, or an argument with your little sister. Like hitting a key basket or playing an instrument, repetition makes it a habit (you'll see how to make this work in chapter 3). You eventually get to the point where mindfulness happens right when you most need it.

But don't take our word for it—try for yourself. See if you find it useful. We are confident you will, and the same goes for self-compassion.

How Can Self-Compassion Help?

Self-compassion means being kind to yourself, particularly when you're struggling. Being supportive of yourself steers you toward feeling resilient and confident. We all benefit from it, but when you have ADHD, self-compassion is particularly important. Teens are hard on themselves overall, and teens with ADHD tend to be especially hard on themselves. As we already mentioned, that makes it even tougher to get anything done.

Self-compassion has three parts:

- **mindfulness**—being aware of your thoughts, feelings, and bodily sensations, without freaking out

- **common humanity**—understanding that like all human beings, you're going to struggle sometimes

- **self-kindness**—taking an active step by being supportive and doing something nice for yourself

When you put this together, self-compassion means that when you feel bad, you treat yourself with the same gentleness that you would treat a good friend. Let's look at what that means in your life.

Mindfulness, Self-Compassion, and ADHD

I realized one day how often I'm angry at myself. I get frustrated when I try something and know what I want to do and then I don't do it anyway. When I can say nicer things to myself, I feel better for sure and I also get more stuff done.

—Julio, age 13

When you practice mindfulness, you see better how your thoughts work. You learn, for example, that the annoying voices inside your head telling you you're stupid, or a failure, are simply thoughts, not facts. You don't have to take them seriously.

Seeing that your habitual nasty voice is not based in reality is mindfulness. Most people feel better and work harder when letting go of this self-criticism.

Giving less attention to your inner critical voice is a first step toward enjoying life more. It's easy to get caught up in negativity and to miss what you're doing well. We all get lost in worrying about what might be coming next, or what we did last week, and that pattern changes how we feel. For example, when caught up in past or future thinking, we overlook fun moments and don't enjoy them as much.

But there is another possibility. When you are feeling down on yourself and like everyone is mad at you, turn toward self-compassion. You don't have to feel good about whatever happened, but you can treat yourself with respect while working your way through. As you would do for a friend in that moment, move yourself toward a realistic and kind attitude: *I messed up. That happens, but now I'm back on track and I'm going to work on it.*

Being kinder to yourself does not mean you're off the hook about getting done what you were supposed to get done. In other words, you still have to figure out how to complete that assignment. But while you catch up, you don't need to beat yourself up for leaving it until the last minute—again.

If that goal sounds odd, consider that everyone from actors to athletes gets better when they allow themselves to bounce back from mistakes instead of dwelling on them. Yep, stuff happens, you flubbed your line, that feels awful—but comfort yourself as best as you're able, and get up and try again.

So how do you do that? The answer is self-compassion. The next time you are upset, follow the steps in the next exercise, which shows you how to give yourself a moment of kindness when you're struggling. You can act in a way that's kind to yourself and other people, is constructive, and gets things done. Try it now, and you'll have a useful practice to use when you need it.

FORMAL PRACTICE: **A Moment for Me**[3]

Consider this practice right when something rattles you. Maybe an adult is upset with you, you did poorly on a test, or you left your lunch at home—for the third time this week. If nothing upsets you right now, think of a time in the past. Close your eyes, and imagine how you felt while this situation happened.

Do this practice slowly, aiming to feel the feelings and meaning behind the words. You can download an audio recording at https://www.newharbinger .com/46394.

First, say to yourself, slowly and patiently: *In this moment, a part of me is struggling.*

This is mindfulness, being aware of what you're feeling. You could also say, *Whoa, this feels awful,* or *This sucks,* or maybe *This is stressful.*

Now say to yourself: *Struggling is a part of life.*

This is common humanity, knowing that others struggle too. You could say, *I'm not alone feeling this,* or *All teens feel this at some time or another.*

Now, say to yourself: *May I be kind to myself.*

This is the self-kindness part of self-compassion. As a teen, you are going through many transitions. Your brain is changing, your body is changing. Maybe you're shifting your friend group.

Ask yourself, *What do I need to hear right now?* If words don't come to you right away, ask yourself, *What would I say to a good friend who was going through this? Can I wish the same for myself?* Commonly used phrases that capture that wish include:

May I give myself the compassion that I need.

May I accept myself as I am.

May I begin to learn how to accept myself as I am.

May I forgive myself.

May I be strong.

May I be safe.

May I be peaceful.

May I know that I deserve love.

If the "May I" feels strange to you or like you are asking permission, you can leave that out and say, *I wish to accept myself just as I am,* or even nothing more than *Be strong* or *Accept myself.*

Now take a few moments to say these words over and over slowly to yourself. Remember to feel the meaning behind the words. The words aren't as important as what they represent. Allow yourself to hear these good wishes for yourself. Soak up these words like a sponge.

Notice how you feel now at the practice's end. Maybe you feel a little better, calmer, or safer. Or maybe not, and it all felt weird. If that was true, have no fear. With time, practicing self-compassion feels much more comfortable. We promise!

Whatever happens in life, if we can see what's going on and act from a place of compassion, we'll know what makes sense to try next. Once you're settled and feeling more resilient, it's easier to make a new study schedule, or remember to call a friend, or do whatever else you need to do. You'll feel more relaxed, and when you are, it's easier to keep track of everything. That's one reason mindfulness and self-compassion directly help you take control of your ADHD.

Sometimes, being told to be mindful can seem judgmental. It's like someone has implied that if you work hard enough with mindfulness, you won't have ADHD anymore. Which isn't true. ADHD isn't your fault, and you can't make it go away through effort alone. But that's not why to try mindfulness.

Mindfulness *does* help with focus, but also lots more. Quite usefully, mindfulness helps decrease stress and anxiety—something we're all quite familiar with. You may feel it even more, because ADHD is an anxiety-producing disorder; it's harder to keep up with whatever you need to be doing. While swamped by your ADHD, it's harder to figure out what to do about it. Who makes a good decision when overly stressed? Fortunately, mindfulness helps a lot with ADHD, stress, and emotions in particular. That lets you manage your life with more ease.

That's important, because ADHD is not something most people outgrow. Your symptoms probably will get better, because your brain will continue to mature until you are about twenty-five years old. ADHD also gets much better if you stay on top of treating it. In addition to mindfulness and self-compassion practices, that may include supports inside and outside of school, health and lifestyle choices, and possibly even medication.

Okay, you've been reading a bunch. It's important to take breaks regularly for your mind and for your body too! So take a break. We move all the time, but how often do we pay attention to how that feels? More often, we stay lost in thought, distractedly off somewhere else in our mind.

FORMAL PRACTICE: **Mindful Movement**

Right now, bring your attention to whatever you are feeling in your body. Are you relaxed, sore, jittery, or warm? Maybe something else? What's going on in your body right now?

Then consider, what does your body need? To move? Or to stretch? Maybe to jump up and down? Maybe you feel like shaking your body all over or doing some yoga. Whatever you choose, pay attention to exactly how movement feels right now in your body.

As best as you're able, consider what changes as you move. What do you notice where your feet touch the floor? What parts feel better? Do any feel worse?

Noticing how your body feels is mindfulness, in a natural way exploring your moment-to-moment experience. Taking a minute to move in whatever way feels good to you is an act of self-compassion.

Summing It Up

You didn't make your ADHD. But you can make a plan that moves yourself past the point where it affects you as much. And part of your plan can be treating yourself as you would a good friend. Consider again how you would advise a friend about learning piano, or recovering from an injury, or learning any new skill. You would encourage them with empathy and tell them they were doing great even if they made the tiniest improvement.

You can do the same for yourself. Each time you make small progress, instead of focusing on what you haven't yet done, start with words of encouragement.

Over time, you will learn to handle ADHD better on your own, and to recognize when to reach out for support too. With that, you will become more independent and successful, happily steering your life forward. Mindfulness and self-compassion practices get you into the right frame of mind to build useful habits that move you behind the wheel— permanently. Then all you have to do is step on the gas and drive.

You can read this book straight through or take it one chapter, or even a half-chapter, at a time. If you run into ideas or concepts that interest you, or ones that feel challenging, talk them through with someone you trust. And then find the chapters that seem important to use as a reference whenever something feels difficult. Remember, you're in the driver's seat. It's all up to you.

CHAPTER 2

Waking Up Your Sleepy Brain Manager

Everyone thought I was lazy and didn't care. I did everything last minute, always forgetting things and running back to school. My grades weren't great and I felt dumb. Then we figured out my ADHD. My grades went up, and I stopped blaming myself for having a hard time keeping track of things.

—Marisa, age 17

If you want to accomplish your goals, you have to know how ADHD affects *your* plans specifically. Once you see how ADHD keeps you from doing what you want, you can make the changes you need.

For starters, ADHD isn't only about inattention or hyperactivity. Yes, it's confusing. After all, it *is* called attention deficit hyperactivity disorder. But that's only how we used to understand it. The best way to think about ADHD now is that it affects a group of mental abilities called our *executive function*. These are all the skills we use that help us keep track of our goals, make long-term plans, and exercise our best judgment.

Think of executive function as your brain manager. It's like how a sports team needs a manager who gets all the players to play well together. Or if you prefer, like an orchestra needs a conductor to coordinate how the musicians make music together. Even if the group members are great, the group still needs a strong leader.

In the same way, our brain manager (meaning, our executive function) is responsible for managing how we achieve our goals. When the brain manager isn't working fully, it may be hard to focus even when you know you "should." Or you may act impulsively even though you know better. Or you may not figure out the best long-term solution to a problem, and grab instead at the first idea that comes to mind.

So let's look at everything you and your brain manager have to manage: Schoolwork, of course. Also your social life, and conversations. And your emotions. Your calendar, health, and situations like driving a car. Unfortunately, anything having to do with managing your life can be impacted by ADHD.

Yet this fact means nothing else about who you are. Like everyone, you have skills that come easily for you. You may be good at math, helpful, or creative. And like everyone, you have other skills that are harder for you. With ADHD, that happens to be "managing" your plans.

So let's look at the way your unique brain manager works. Once you understand that, you will know how to better accomplish whatever you want to do.

Mapping Out the Brain Manager[4]

The brain manager has a lot to do. Here we'll look at some of what ADHD often impacts. You probably don't experience all of what's described below, since everyone's ADHD is different, but notice what you can relate to. This awareness will help you bring your brain manager back to task.

Management of Attention

Attention—or being aware of what is going on at any given moment—is a complicated skill to understand. When you're managing your attention well, you hear what the teacher is saying; for example, you register whatever is assigned and work without getting distracted. You transition your attention smoothly between one point of focus (like something you're reading) and another (like registering that your teacher is telling you it's time to move on). ADHD is not always about poor focus; it's about using your attention well.

What this may mean for you: When you have ADHD, you may over-focus on some things (particularly fun ones) to the point where you lose track of time. When things get difficult, it's often hard to pay attention at all. That's when adults assume you don't care. But you do care; it's just hard to focus and follow through. At other times, it's hard to shift your attention between two things (like the TV and your mom talking), which can make people believe you aren't listening to them.

Management of Behavior

This is the clichéd stereotype of ADHD—the kid who can't sit still, or who acts and speaks without thinking. Yet half of people with ADHD don't have hyperactivity or impulsiveness. Acting or speaking before thinking can be anything from disruptive (like talking out of turn in a classroom) to dangerous (like being the first to jump off a high wall).

What this may mean for you: It feels terrible to realize, right after it happens, that you've been impulsive. *I shouldn't have said that. I shouldn't have eaten all the donuts.* Sometimes that leads us to cover up what we did or get angry at someone else. And then we feel even worse!

Management of Tasks

ADHD makes it hard to organize yourself, create plans, and keep track of time. As you grow older, this can be the hardest part of ADHD to deal with.

What this may mean for you: This is key to ADHD: Don't think about it as an attention problem alone. It is often a time management and keeping-track-of-your-goals problem.

Management of Information

On a computer, there are two types of memory, the hard drive and the RAM. The hard drive stores facts, and the RAM coordinates actions live. Your brain is similar. You may know a ton, like memorizing the manual for your driver's test. Your brain manager is the RAM using that information while navigating road signs, directions, people, and other cars. With ADHD, that means it gets hard to do things like take notes during lectures or remember a list of what you need to do.

What this may mean for you: Life is easier if you start moving toward an attitude of "Either I'm doing it right now, or I will make myself a reminder to do it right now." Avoid putting added pressure on yourself by trying to keep track of things in your head. Write them down.

Management of Effort

Working hard, which you are probably doing already, is different from sustaining effort, like keeping at a task or project all the way to the end without getting distracted or losing interest. It's like sprinters and long-distance runners. For folks with ADHD, maintaining a long-distance run is not so easy. Staying motivated from beginning to end of a long-term task is hard with ADHD.

What this may mean for you: You aim to keep working and regardless, find yourself distracted and off-task, which can be completely frustrating. But you can learn ways to keep your brain manager awake and on task. We'll show you how later in this book.

Management of Emotions

Of course, emotions are part of life, and all of us need to learn to manage them well. With ADHD, emotions take over very quickly. People with ADHD often are quick to get upset or angry, or give up, until they learn ways to handle their emotions.

What this may mean for you: When emotions swamp your thinking, they get in the way of feeling resilient (*I quit!*) or even of relationships (*I hate you!*). An explosion happens, and you recover almost right away while everyone else stays dazed. But there's a difference between the emotion you feel and what you do next. Notice your habits, and you can adjust them over time.

As you can see, ADHD affects more than only school. Which executive function challenges sound familiar? Your brain manager plays a part in nearly everything you do.

You can explore almost any challenge by looking for ways executive function is involved. As you'll see throughout the rest of the book, once you see things that way, new solutions will come to you also (a worksheet that lets you explore problem solving with executive function in mind is available at https://www.newharbinger.com/46394). Consider the six aspects of executive function listed above, see which most applies, and then work on a new plan using that information.

Fortunately, you can get to the point where you don't feel as if ADHD is always in control. For one thing, executive function itself matures and improves all the way into your twenties. And, because you're reading this, you are already ahead of the game. You have taken one huge step forward to living more easily by learning about yourself and ADHD. Take a moment to congratulate yourself!

Of course, you've also finished a whole lot of reading about ADHD. So let's take a moment to rest your mind before going further. In the following mindfulness exercise, you will learn an effective way to calm your busy mind, and to recognize what is going on in this very moment.

INFORMAL PRACTICE: Three Mindful Breaths

This practice is great for helping you settle if you feel edgy or off. You can do it anytime you feel a little agitated, upset, frustrated, or bored. Three slow breaths to get in touch with what is happening and decide what to do next. It takes less than ten seconds.

Right where you are, find the place in your body where you can most easily feel your breath. This may be the tip of your nose, or your mouth. It could be the feeling of your chest or belly as your lungs expand and contract with each breath.

Now take one breath, and feel how your body moves.

Notice the small pause between your in-breath and your out-breath, and then again at the end of your out-breath before the next in-breath starts.

Do this for three breaths.

If you notice your mind wandering at any time, gently bring your attention back to feeling your breath.

Going forward, you can do this practice anytime you feel unsettled.

I had been trying to write an essay for history, and the topic was so boring—about why I thought the explorers wanted to explore. I mean, who cares and how should I know? I couldn't think of anything—except that my friends wanted to go outside to ride bikes. I was ready to tear up my homework. So I did my three breaths. Then I decided to go for another three. I was able to get back to the essay, at least for a little while.

—Jake, age 12

Navigating ADHD with (Self) Care

When you have ADHD, your brain manager—responsible for supervising and making things happen—is not yet totally engaged. Because of that, you may hit some potholes, situations where you saw what "should" have happened or what you "should" have done, but didn't.

As we mentioned in the previous chapter, many of us, when we make a mistake, immediately start thinking self-critical thoughts: *I blew it again. I'm such a loser.* That type of negative thinking makes it harder to rally and figure out what to do next.

We're biologically wired to pay more attention to the negative things that we encounter, which might harm us, than the positive ones, which won't. Our negative thoughts tend to stay in our minds when things don't go our way. *I always screw up. I can't ever make my parents happy.* This is called *negativity bias.* A zillion years ago, when we lived out in the wild, we had to be aware of things, like predators, that could hurt us.

Of course, we're not exactly out in the wilderness anymore. What our brain thinks of as harmful, like being late to class or being criticized by adults, isn't usually life-threatening. Still, when these things happen, our brain behaves as though we're still out in the wilderness, and our inner critic speaks up to tell us what we did wrong, or could have done better, or should have thought of but didn't. And over time, it has a huge effect on our self-confidence and self-image.

I intend to keep my room clean. I really do. I start, and the next thing I know I'm on the floor looking through some random book. Then I feel bad, because I promised my dad I would clean, and on top of that, now I have to rush through my homework. I try to do what I'm supposed to, and I mess up. I feel bad about myself a lot of the time.

—Roxy, age 14

But here's the thing: Right in a moment of struggle, you can pause when you notice yourself getting down on yourself. And then choose to behave in a way that's kinder to yourself. That doesn't mean that you are "excused" from fixing your mistakes, but you don't have to add to the situation by beating yourself up. Instead, you can remind yourself that everyone messes up, you're doing the best you can, and there's no need to be quite so self-critical.

One thing that helps is self-compassion. In fact, you practiced it already in "A Moment for Me." You practice kindness for yourself in difficult moments, which makes it easier to focus on doing things better next time.

Next you will learn another way to combat the common habit of self-criticism: remembering what you know you are good at. Keeping in mind what you're good at can help you stay resilient under stress.

FORMAL PRACTICE: **Knowing What I'm Good At**[5]

This is a great exercise to do daily, maybe when you wake up or go to bed. It takes only a couple of minutes and helps you stay in touch with whatever is going well even on days things feel hard. You'll find an audio recording to follow at https://www.newharbinger.com/46394.

Find a comfortable place to sit or lie down.

Close your eyes, and take a few deep breaths to allow yourself to relax.

Now shifting your attention, think about something you appreciate about yourself. That you fully, deep down, like about yourself. It could be liking the way you draw, or that you're good at video games, or are awesome on a skateboard. You won't have to share with anyone, so you can be honest.

Sometimes it's easier to appreciate ourselves when we remember that our good qualities often come from the positive influences of other people in our lives. Maybe you've learned video games from a friend, or you're good at drawing because someone in your family encourages you. Think of people who have had a positive impact on you, maybe parents or caregivers, teachers, friends, or even authors of books. As you consider each one, imagine sending them some appreciation.

Now, let yourself enjoy this moment of feeling good about yourself. Let it soak in. Remember, you don't have to be the best at anything or perfect to appreciate something about yourself.

Stay with this practice for as long as you'd like, and when you're ready, gently open your eyes.

Take a moment to compare how you're feeling right now to before doing this exercise. You may already feel a bit better about yourself.

The fact that you have ADHD doesn't change the good things about you, even though it can feel like no one else sees them yet. Although it's easy to remember the negative stuff, we can make a habit of remembering the positive too. When we do, we'll feel less anxiety and more at ease. We build something real to hang on to and help us cope when things get difficult.

So, take a moment to remind yourself of the good things about you. Enjoy and celebrate them, and come back to them when life feels rough. It's not that easy, so we encourage you to practice often!

Recognizing How Your ADHD Makes You Think

One trick to consider when you have ADHD is approaching any difficulty as if it *all* has to do with your brain manager. That is, challenge any belief you have that things are hard because you're not good enough, or that you'll never change. Neither is true, but your ADHD may make you feel that way.

What if a hard situation is challenging *entirely because of your ADHD?* You could assume it's just you, and that there's no way you could study any better for that math test or figure out a way to keep track of all your homework. You might hear adults tell you things like, "Come on, if you cared enough, you'd write down what's due. What's so hard about that?" Or you might tell yourself things like, *This should be easy. I can't believe I forgot which books to bring home again.* But even writing down your homework is harder than it seems, especially with ADHD.

In reality, it takes many steps for your brain manager to complete the task of writing down homework. Remember, ADHD isn't only attention and behavior. It's also keeping track of time and all the details in your life. So, for the *supposedly* simple task of recording your homework, your brain handles all of this:

- Managing your emotions and staying calm

- Paying attention when your teacher says something important

- Avoiding a distracting conversation, or ignoring an urge to be at lunch, that would make you miss what the teacher said

- Knowing where your day planner and pen are

- Quickly getting to the right page for writing the assignment down before leaving the room

- Avoiding the urge to write it down later

- Remembering the details to write down

The reality is you probably *know* how to write your homework down and finish it, get along with others, and stay healthy. Your ADHD sometimes steers you the wrong way. Even when you promise yourself to manage your schoolwork better, your brain manager slips up and you lose track again. Looking at it as a problem with executive function, you can find new solutions for yourself.

The ADHD part of you also may tell you to put off your homework to the last minute, or make you forget to start at all. In addition to making it hard to focus, your ADHD says, "Homework is boring, and I'm tired. It can wait." Rather than blaming yourself, or assuming you can't change, how about saying, *Ah, that's my ADHD talking... I don't have to listen, though. I can make a healthier choice.* Your ADHD symptoms are real, but they also may influence the choices you make.

One way to think of it is that it's only the ADHD part of you that pushes back, not your own wisest self. You may hate to-do lists and time management and organization only because they don't "work well" for you yet. *Yeah,* you might think, *I don't really keep a calendar. Not my thing.* Except that the reason these tools don't "work," and feel uncomfortable, is that you have ADHD in the first place.

ADHD sometimes undermines the exact plans needed to manage ADHD. It's like it both causes something to be hard for you, and then causes the easiest solution to seem wrong to you. In reality, you *can* keep a to-do list or a calendar, or find a way to keep track of your life. Consider how your brain manager might make these tasks difficult (but that doesn't mean they're impossible). This may sound too hard or abstract for now. Don't worry; making this happen is what the rest of this book covers.

A Quick Check-In with Yourself

As you read, notice any reactions you're having, like wanting to throw this book across the room. Or denying you have ADHD at all. Or feeling annoyed that you need to do something different.

Those are all normal thoughts.

For now, when these thoughts show up, simply notice them. Then say something to yourself like: *That's my brain manager, asleep at the wheel. I'm not going to let it hijack my life. I'm going to do what's best for me.* Rather than acting on your first impulse, come back and read more. Maybe do the three breaths practice you learned in this chapter. Acknowledge any restlessness you feel, and let it pass. Then make a careful decision about what to do next.

Also take care of yourself. If you feel like you've read enough, take a break. Shoot a few baskets, go for a run, put on music and dance—whatever floats your boat. You can do this whenever you feel it's impossible to keep your brain manager on task for a bit. Just make sure you come back to your goal of reading the book and practicing the skills when you can.

And…

Know that once you understand your brain manager better, you'll know how to more effectively work with it. You'll learn how to be in control of what you do, rather than your ADHD.

Now that you've checked in with your needs, let's turn back to recognizing your ADHD in action.

ADHD, Stress, and Taking Back Control

Your state of mind affects how you act. That's common sense. When happy and calm, you'll behave differently than when stressed and overwhelmed.

ADHD itself makes life more stressful. It may take you longer than everyone else to finish your work. You forget details in schoolwork and scramble at the last minute to recover. That brain manager is asleep at the wheel, slow to figure what you need to do, and leaves you stuck here, juggling everyday life.

Over time, maybe you get burned out. And then how you act affects not only you, but also those around you. You react without thinking. And not surprisingly, treating others that way leads to more stress for you.

When we're too stressed, we're not at our best. Pressure from school, parents on our backs, assignments, or responsibilities—it all causes us to start up our self-defense network. Fight-flight-freeze is a biological system that helps us respond to danger. It sets us up to attack, run away, or hide. Feeling threatened kicks off our defenses; our stress hormones increase, and we feel it in our bodies.

That process is important when we're really in danger. But in modern life we're often living in this fight-flight-freeze state even when perfectly safe. We may be struggling academically or having trouble with a friend. Our fight-flight-freeze system kicks in again, but we're not at *actual* physical risk. And yet, our bodies react just the same.

In moments of real life-threatening danger, we want to quickly get to safety. Outside of a true emergency, that urge often leads to choices that we regret. Those poor choices increase our stress all over again. The cycle continues, but we're just trying to prepare for a math test.

Being stressed causes an escalating cycle of *more* stress. Feeling emotionally off pushes our ability to think clearly and sends us even further into orbit. Then thoughts trigger stressful feelings. That cycle may even change how we sleep and how we feel physically. And that makes us more stressed again. Which again changes how we think, and act.

I was feeling pretty good about my presentation, right until I realized I left my notecards on the kitchen table. Class was starting and I panicked. My heart was racing, and my head started to pound. I knew that the teacher would think I hadn't done my work. I could feel myself about to cry. I ran down the hallway in the opposite direction of class and hid in the girls' bathroom. But then, I got in trouble for skipping class.

—Sarah, age 16

Once Sarah's fight-flight-freeze system activated, her stress took over. She made a choice in the heat of the moment that was understandable but also not the best in the long run. What might have happened differently if Sarah was able to pause before acting? Perhaps she could have remained calm and spoken to the teacher about her situation, or found another alternative.

To stay flexible in how we live, think, and solve problems, we must step out of the stress cycle. Lower your stress and everything else gets easier. And how do we lower stress? We lower it by (1) staying fully aware—mindful—of our experience as it happens, like sensations in our body, (2) staying compassionate with ourselves, and (3) making wise decisions about how to act so that we'll choose the healthiest thing for ourselves in the long run.

Solving Problems with Self-Compassion

I've found that there are no secret solutions, but everything is better when I remember to be mindful and compassionate toward myself. I mean, sometimes it feels soul crushing to try and try, and it feels like nothing works or sticks long enough and nothing ever changes. I want to curl up and quit. But when I remember self–compassion, I can keep at it even when it seems boring and like it should work easily. Everything does keep getting better, now that I'm not so hard on myself.

—Jennifer, age 17

If a friend starred on the swim team and hurt her shoulder, you'd proba- bly offer her emotional support. You'd say something like, "Oh, that's awful! Can I maybe carry your backpack?" You'd also encourage her to do whatever work has to get done in the gym to get back to full strength. And yet for ourselves, if *we* hurt our shoulder, both the prospect of going to the gym and the disappointment of missing swim season might over- whelm us.

It's common to live life one way though we'd recommend something entirely different for someone else. It can be helpful to consider what you'd suggest to a friend in the same situation.

What would you recommend for a friend having a hard time with ADHD? For starters, ADHD affects planning. What attitude would you encourage for a friend who was challenged with planning a project?

As you're starting to learn, your ADHD can prevent you from living the life you *want* to live. Having ADHD means that you struggle to com- plete certain things that others seem to do easily—or at least without as much stress. When this happens, your negative voice starts chattering.

"You're such an idiot! You'll never be good at anything!" Inside that spin, it's hard to stay motivated. So it can be useful to imagine exactly what you'd tell a good friend: "Yeah, I don't like asking teachers for help either, but if you're going to pass that class you probably should go to office hours."

Self-compassion requires exactly this: talking to yourself as you would talk to a good friend. Mindfulness teacher Sharon Salzberg calls self-compassion our main engine for change. Switching to that power source requires no special equipment. All you need is yourself. It's one huge step toward taking the wheel back from ADHD and taking care of what you need more easily.

With that in mind, let's try another exercise. In this exercise, you're going to imagine that your good friend has ADHD and see what you might say to him.

EXERCISE: **How Would I Treat a Friend?** [6]

Imagine that a good friend with ADHD forgot about a big science test and didn't study. As a result, he did poorly. He felt terrible about himself. He came to you and expressed how upset he was about his grade and forgetting to study. On a piece of paper, write down how you might respond to your friend. What would you say? What would your tone of voice be?

If you're like most teens, you might say something like, "Oh, I'm so sorry! I know how you feel. That's happened to me. It's so hard to remember everything, but I'm sure you can fix it. Let's go hang out and talk about it." You'd comfort him and sort out what to do next so he remembers to study next time.

Now, imagine that this situation happened to you. Imagine you forgot about the science test, didn't study, and got a bad grade. Now…

What would you say to yourself? What words would you say and what tone of voice would you use? Write this down, too.

If you are like most people, you probably would say some self-critical things like, *I'm so stupid! I screwed up AGAIN! The teacher's been talking about it for two weeks! Why can't I keep track of these things?! Ugh! I'm such a jerk!*

How is your advice for your friend similar to or different from how you usually treat yourself? What would it be like if next time you have a problem you say to yourself the same words that you said to your friend? Rather than putting yourself down, say something like, *Oh, I'm so sorry this happened. It's hard to remember stuff, especially with ADHD. I know you're trying really hard. But this is hard, so be patient!*

It might seem weird to talk to yourself this way, but try it. What can it hurt? See if that shift in perspective—what would I tell a friend right now?—makes it easier to figure out what to do next.

Summing It Up

Mindfulness helps us recognize when we're struggling and when we're not being kind to ourselves. And then, with self-compassion, we treat ourselves better, like we would a good friend. Self-compassion also recognizes that we deserve to live our lives without beating ourselves up so much. That's more practical than it seems; it allows you to stay on target as you navigate whatever you face day to day, whether it's paying attention in class, getting homework finished, or cleaning your room.

How can you make mindfulness and self-compassion an integral part of your life, and how can you develop better habits around your ADHD? The next chapter will explain…

CHAPTER 3

Developing Habits That Stick

I used to push myself so hard playing tennis. I played harder than anyone around me, but then, when I made a mistake, I'd blow up at myself. I once even smashed my racket against a wall when I blew a serve. I kept melting down during tough matches. I'd miss a couple of shots, and then that voice would start heckling, like, *Here you go again, falling apart when it matters.* At one point, I was ready to quit tennis. But now I remind myself, *Don't worry, everyone misses a serve sometimes.* I'm human! I take a few breaths, feel the ground beneath my feet, and set myself for the next point. Now playing tennis is a whole lot more fun.

—Nico, age 15

With mindfulness, we wake up to how we live our lives. Otherwise, we make many choices habitually—mindlessly—without giving them our full attention. That's true with or without ADHD. When off-balance and caught up in fear, anger, or distraction, we don't see all the ways we act out of habit.

On the other hand, when mindful and aware, we consciously guide ourselves toward feeling more happy, resilient, and independent. It starts with catching ourselves when lost in a less-than-useful mental habit, like believing our inner critic, and steering back to what's actually happening in real time.

What's more, changing the mental habit of self-criticism allows us to change other habits. When we are patient with ourselves, we can find ways to manage our time or respond to difficult people in our lives with skill. We can make sure we're always the one in the driver's seat.

We know ADHD is a challenge. It can get in the way of much of what you want. Taking control starts with figuring out in which areas of life ADHD affects *you*.

Thinking of ADHD that way means it is not a judgment of who you are. Look at it as seeking skills to sharpen that will make your life easier. Change habits that aren't working out, build new habits *you* choose, and become the person *you* want to be.

We'll start our journey of habit change with another look at how our overly obnoxious, self-critical voice inside gets in the way of our best intentions.

Getting to Know Your Inner Critic

Consider what happens when you make a mistake. You probably hear an inner voice saying something like, "You forgot to hand in the assignment...again? What's wrong with you?" That easily turns into a mental spin-off, as anger and frustration build and take over, possibly making it less likely you'll succeed the next time. Which might set the same cycle off again, until you recognize the pattern and step out of it.

Is there a purpose to that voice we call our inner critic? Often, people say it motivates them or keeps them in line. On some level, we believe this harshness is necessary for remembering to hand in our assignments.

"Hey, dummy, whatever you do, don't forget again." In reality, we know from research that a harsh critic doesn't make us more successful or motivated, it only makes us feel worse about ourselves.[7]

Too much self-criticism eventually makes us want to give up. We lose motivation. We make one mistake, and that voice says, "Don't bother. You'll never get it." And when we feel bad about ourselves, we sometimes treat others badly. Which doesn't help their life, or ours. So we end up less happy and resilient when our critic wins.

What can you do instead? Start seeing that critic as only *one* part of you, like your ADHD is. It is one piece of you that you don't necessarily need to listen to so much.

Rather than letting your inner critic tell you you're such an airhead because you forgot to finish your math homework yesterday, remember there's also a wise, compassionate part of you. You may not feel like it, but you can learn to pay more attention to that supportive voice instead of the self-critical one.

You meant to hand in the assignment, but you forgot. Everyone forgets things sometimes. Let that wise voice speak. "Oh no, not again! That hurts, but it's going to be okay." Know that like every other imperfect human being on the planet, you deserve kindness.

Then go out and do something proactive. Ask someone to remind you to write down today's assignment in your planner. And then program a reminder in your phone that will remind you to hand it in online before you go to sleep.

Finally, give yourself credit. Pat yourself on the back for the small steps you've taken. For most of us, the most realistic way to change is one small step at a time. Remember, your ADHD is part of what makes you the unique, interesting person that you are. And yet, there is always more you can do to learn and to make your life a little easier. That's one way self-compassion can help you grow.

Now, let's practice how to replace the habit of self-criticism with a more constructive one.

EXERCISE: **Working with Your Inner Critic**[8]

You can download an audio recording of this exercise at https://www.newharbinger.com/46394.

Think of some behavior that you continue to beat yourself up about and write it down: for example, "I don't finish my homework" or "I forget to do my chores" or "I can be irritable with my parents or siblings."

Now write down what your inner critic typically says when this happens, including its tone of voice. Take a moment to consider how much suffering that inner critic has caused you.

If you like, comfort yourself by saying a few kind phrases to yourself. Maybe something like: *I'm sorry this is so hard!* Or *You are dealing with so much—it's tough having ADHD!* Or *You'll get through this!*

Take a moment to consider whether your inner critic is trying to protect you in some way, even if it's unproductive. This is a part of you that wants you to do well. If you feel that your critic is trying to protect you in some way, write down how.

Sometimes, our inner critic *doesn't* feel at all useful, like the criticism has no value. If that's the case, keep saying the reassuring words to yourself—not because that changes how you feel, but because you're hurting.

That was a lot! Before going on, take three mindful breaths. Settle down and take a breather. Then move on when you're feeling ready.

Now let's hear from another part of you. Just like you have a habitual critical voice, you also have a kinder, gentler voice, the voice of your more compassionate self. This voice sounds like someone who loves you completely and accepts you fully. We all have a kinder, gentler voice inside, though it may be pretty well hidden.

What might that compassionate part of you say right now? Maybe something like:

"I know how hard it is being a teen. You're dealing with so much and you're doing what you can right now."

"ADHD can make life more challenging, but it will all be okay."

"I care about you and I don't want you to struggle so much!"

If you have a hard time finding kind words to say, that's normal. Consider again what a good friend might say, or even a pet (if you have one). Pets often seem quite empathetic and know when we need them. If they could talk, they might say something like, *You're the best, I'm here for you, now scratch my ears.*

Take time to silently repeat this kinder message to yourself. Let your kind words sink in.

Now, write yourself a brief letter using the voice of your compassionate self.

What positive words might encourage you to change this habit that you beat yourself up about? Does your more compassionate self have any ideas? For example, maybe the words "I really care about you and don't want you to struggle" would help you feel less angry with yourself for shouting out in class.

If you've found some new words coming from this kinder voice, enjoy the feeling of being supported. But if you are having trouble finding the words, that's okay too. It may take some time. Learn at your pace, with self-compassion. Give the message time to sink in.

We know that when our kind voice grows and our inner critic quiets, we feel better, work harder, and treat other people better too. That thoughtful voice inside us guides us far more skillfully than a perfectionistic, harsh one.

Your self-compassionate voice wants you to be successful because it cares for you. Treating ourselves with kindness doesn't mean we don't have stuff to work on. Of course, we do. But we don't have to continually beat ourselves up to get that work done. So as a place to start, how about aiming to listen to your nicer voice for a change?

How do your inner critic, mindfulness, and self-compassion relate to ADHD? It's a whole lot easier to put effort into making life easier when you truly value yourself. Recognize that your inner critic isn't telling you the truth, and you can stop paying so much attention to it. Self-compassion allows for that. It's valuable to understand that while thoughts often *feel* like facts, they're nothing more than thoughts.

Thoughts Are Not Facts

Mindfulness teaches you to notice thoughts without taking for granted that you need to believe each one. *I'm the worst* is an idea, a reflex, and far different from *I feel bad I made a mistake, but everyone does. What should I do now?*

Mindfulness means seeing life clearly. We notice what we think, including what we believe. Instead of getting caught up in all our thoughts, we consider whether they are true or not.

Is *everything* you think true? Say there's a difficult test coming up in math. Before you know it, you jump on a train of worrying thoughts: *I'm going to fail this test and then the class and then not get into college and my whole life will be ruined.* What *is* true is that the test may be hard, that's all. The thoughts that follow are a mental spin-off, not facts.

Our minds create thoughts all the time. *How come penguins don't fly and I have to pick up milk for Mom and wow that new kid is cute and maybe we'll go to the prom together wait is that the ice cream truck?* Some are useful, like remembering the milk for Mom. Many are not, like getting lost in anxiety before a test even when we prepared. And even if we aren't all that well prepared, getting lost in stressful thinking doesn't help anyway.

Furthermore, thoughts often steer us into concerns about the future or fretting about the past. They lead us to frustrating places that rev up our stress. It's one thing to learn from the past, or to plan for the future. It's another thing entirely to get lost in one or both.

A research study showed that when your mind wanders (in other words, when you are being mind*less*), you tend to stress about things you already did or dread what might happen next. You're less happy than when you stay aware of what you're actually doing. In other words, when we're not mindful, we tend to worry and stress. When we are mindful, we're happier.[9]

So what does this have to do with living differently? When you're lost in thought, you're not attending to what you're doing. If it's time for homework, and your mind wanders to your favorite video game, that makes it more likely you're going to rush, or forget to do a step, or leave your homework on the kitchen table. But then if you're mindful when you pack your backpack, you'll check off every item you need—pen, paper, books—and every assignment that should go back to school. So your homework isn't only done, it's handed in. There's no way that all can happen if your mind wanders off to tomorrow's soccer game while you're packing.

It's hard to change how we think through effort and desire alone. For example, people often say things like, "Stop being hard on yourself." While that's useful advice, it's not easy to do without the right tools. Mindfulness is one of the tools you need, so let's try another practice. This is a teen favorite—it's simple, easy to develop into a habit, and fun!

FORMAL PRACTICE: **Music Meditation**

Quieting your mind is a good first step toward getting on top of your ADHD…or any other challenge.

This next activity shows you how effortless mindfulness can be. It can be as simple as listening to music. Later, we'll use this same practice as an example of how to start a mindfulness routine.

First, pick a piece of instrumental music you find relaxing. Start with music that has no words. Lyrics often get our minds thinking thoughts. If you need them, several suggestions are available online at https://www.newharbinger .com/46394.

What you'll be doing is simply paying attention to the music.

Find a comfortable place to sit or lie down.

Keep your eyes open or closed, whatever feels natural for you.

Start the music.

Pay close attention to each note as the music plays. You could also try focusing on an individual instrument for a while.

You will find your mind has drifted at some point. When this happens, gently—*and without criticizing yourself*—guide your attention back to the

music. While it is easy to think things like, *Blew it again, got distracted...* coming back is what matters. *Nice job, self. I'm back in the music.*

Continue until the music ends—each time you lose track of the music, patiently coming back.

That's it!

How do you feel after listening mindfully to music? If you feel a bit more relaxed, remember you can do this anytime. Put on a piece of music, and instead of staying caught up in thinking, give full attention to the music for a few minutes.

We also bet that your mind wandered quite a bit. Don't worry about that. It doesn't mean that you're doing anything wrong. That's just what our minds do.

It's Not Just You—Everyone Gets Distracted

Mindfulness involves training your mind to come back once it's drifted away. But the mind always wanders off again. We sometimes call it monkey mind because it leaps around constantly. It looks out for anything that could hurt us. Or gets bored and looks for entertainment. In any event, when *your* mind wanders, the instruction is this: notice that it did, and *without judging yourself*, bring yourself back. It's all normal.

People with ADHD often ask if this instruction is for everyone. Their inner critic believes that they are the only ones whose minds wander. But guess what? It turns out monkey mind is true for everyone. Distraction happens for everyone. There's no assumption our thoughts or bodies will ever be fully still. Not for you, not for us, and not for anyone else.

So then you might be thinking, *If I have trouble with focus and sticking to routines because of ADHD in the first place, can I even practice mindfulness?* Yep, you absolutely can.

The one part of mindfulness that is harder with ADHD is remembering to practice, because ADHD makes new routines harder. But if you're distracted while practicing mindfulness, that's normal—with or without ADHD. It doesn't mean you can't do the practice. If it's hard to sit still because you feel fidgety, you don't have to. As we'll get back to later in this book, movement is good. And while it may be harder to remember your new routine than you'd like, if you forget your practice sometimes, that happens to everyone else too. When you remember, simply try again.

Mindfulness calls for awareness without judgment. We more easily notice all the nuances of exactly what is happening. So if you're eating ice cream, you can be mindful of the explosion of coldness and the sweetness of the flavor. That's more fun than what we *all* do quite often, daydreaming and not tasting it, isn't it? If you're listening to music mindfully, you can enjoy the music more fully. And if you're riding your skateboard, being mindful keeps you on your board.

Mindfulness also helps you handle any situation more easily. When we're not paying attention to what's in front of us, we miss details and lose the opportunity to make new choices. That could mean *Homework later, ice cream now*...or of course, *Homework now, ice cream later.* Being mindful means seeing precisely what's going on and actively managing what to do next.

That may sound impossible, but it's like going to the gym. Working out helps us physically; mindfulness helps us mentally. For example, we might decide to build a new habit of pausing before reacting when annoyed. Like any new skill, we won't remember this new habit perfectly every time. But with persistence, over time, we more easily catch ourselves, notice our thoughts, and then decide how we want to relate to whatever is going on in our lives.

In other words, mindfulness puts our brain manager on the job. And we feel less stressed, because we're behind the wheel and managing our life.

I used to get so worked up going into tests I could barely think. And then, if a problem was hard, I'd flip out. I knew I was going to fail. I'd get so angry with myself, like, *Cut it out already, settle down and do the work.* Now I've learned that it's okay to have those thoughts—but I take a little break. I focus on something else for a few breaths. Then I can think again, so I get back to the test.

—Carlos, age 17

Making the Habits You Choose Stick

You're a teenager and deciding how you want to live. A lot of that relies on developing strong habits for yourself. We have ways of getting out the door in the morning. We have ways of dealing with emotions. We have ways of talking to people. All these habits developed over many years.

Having habits is human nature and not inherently right or wrong. Who wants to remember over and over again how to tie our shoes? But if we live *only* out of habit, we get stuck in some unhealthy ruts. Steering our lives requires seeing those habits and actively deciding which to change. That's mindfulness again, staying aware and purposeful in our actions.

New habits are hard to build. Literally, habits hardwire in our brains. Our brains create neurological pathways that become ruts our thoughts fall into. That's both good news and bad all at once: how you live is hard to change once it's hardwired. And yet, new habits are possible because the brain rewires itself based on new experiences.

The brain is like a muscle we train. We can reroute habitual patterns onto new roads. Spend time drawing and painting, and your brain becomes hardwired for those skills. Spend time with video games, and those brain pathways strengthen. And spend time, say, planning your schoolwork for the week in a productive way, and those parts of your brain—your executive function—become more established and more natural for you too.

Because your teenage brain undergoes rapid restructuring and rewiring, it's an ideal time to select your own useful new habits. Some are external habits, like how you get ready for school, while others are more internal. For example, if you're feeling swamped by emotions, you can decide to build up the parts of your brain that make handling emotions easier. That's a pretty radical idea all on its own.

The First Habit to Change: Strengthening Your Mindfulness

You may want to think of ADHD as a goal-setting disorder instead of only as an attention disorder. It's harder to create and stick to your goals. In fact, you need executive function even to handle your own ADHD. How frustrating is that? *Leave me alone, I'm on top of it…* and then your brain manager checks out and you forget anyway. So let's start looking at how you can meet your goals instead.

The effort required to stick to anything new relies on your brain manager. Maybe you want to get better at guitar but never remember to practice. Maybe you want to get a little more sleep but always stay up late anyway. You might want to study more consistently so you can show the world what you're capable of but you get distracted again.

It's useful to make a mindfulness practice one of your *first* new routines. Living with ADHD can make you more stressed, rushed, and irritable, which can get in the way of whatever else you need to do. Mindfulness makes it easier to handle all the rest of managing your ADHD.

That is why we practice mindfulness—not because meditation fixes things, but because of the habits we build while meditating. We develop attention and compassionate awareness of what's going on in our lives. Once mindfulness and self-compassion become habitual, those traits become instinctive in other parts of our lives. Habits we actively choose to reinforce often become permanent and effortless, or at least more familiar and useful for us over time.

Being more mindful and self-aware lets you purposefully reach goals in life. As an example, we'll start with how to make a mindfulness habit stick. These same steps will work for almost any habit, from school to relationships and beyond. But for now, remember that being more mindful will guide you wherever you want to go in any part of your life.

What might a mindfulness habit look like? First, let's explore proven steps for creating any new habit.

Start with a specific plan. Figure out what you want to change and take one small step in that direction. For instance, you want *a regular practice of mindfulness.* That's your goal. So you might do an informal mindfulness practice, like the three breaths practice, before bed. Bedtime already happens every night, so that makes the plan feasible to start.

Staying resilient and independent requires setting realistic goals, but be sure to take small steps. Trying to change everything all at once leads to frustration and makes you less likely to succeed. Expecting to change your behavior perfectly, 100 percent of the time, often leads to frustration and self-criticism once you inevitably fall back into your old habits. But finding one small step to take is something most of us can manage.

Remember to be self-compassionate. Yes, there's a habit you're trying to change. And yes, coming up with a schedule will help you practice. Still, actually sticking with it will be hard. Hearing your kind voice, especially when life gets hard and your inner critic loud, helps with habit change because you won't feel defeated so easily. It's like having an inner coach rooting for you all the way!

If you forget your mindfulness practice one day, even with your reminder, stay compassionate. Forgetting is normal, and the best thing you can do is resolve to try again. Over time, small steps become habitual

and accumulate into bigger changes. Eventually, you might become confident enough around the three breaths practice that you add another formal practice and make your mindfulness habit even stronger.

Connect new habits to old ones. Tie your new habit to something you're already doing so that you do both together. For example, say you always have a snack when you come home from school. You might decide to do the three breaths practice before that snack. This makes it easier for you to remember your new plan every day.

Set up reminders. Until a new habit is ingrained and effortless, it takes reminders to keep practicing. Tricks like these can help you remember to stick to your plan:

Make specific plans, not general ones. For example, don't say, *I'll do my three breaths practice tomorrow.* Say, *I'll do it at 9:00 a.m.* or *I'll do it at bedtime.* This makes it easier to follow through.

Set alarms. Lucky for us, in the digital age reminders are at our fingertips. Don't just *say* you'll practice at 9:00 a.m.; you could forget. Put a reminder in your phone that'll go off right at 9:00, so you remember to practice.

Reward yourself when you remember your new habit. You've finished your homework and put it in your backpack. Now do something healthy that you love—go outside and kick around a soccer ball, take a walk, whatever is enjoyable for you. You deserve it!

Don't be afraid to ask for help keeping yourself on track. Teachers have all kinds of methods to help students keep track of their assignments, like using sticky notes or phone reminders. Or tell a parent that you're going to practice mindfulness before bed and ask for a reminder from them.

We all need help sometimes. In fact, one sign of self-confidence and skill is knowing when to reach out for help, instead of doing everything on our own. One of the largest barriers around reaching out for help is the idea that we don't need or shouldn't ask for help.

Think about airline pilots for a moment. Dozens of time a week, they go over the same preflight checklist. In spite of being close to certain they have done it all, they make a routine of checking over that list with someone else. That's the only way to be sure, and they don't judge themselves for the check-in.

Similarly, we'd probably tell any friend it's no big deal to check in with someone else for support—but for ourselves, we want to show we can take care of everything on our own. Maybe you think, *I shouldn't need help, I'm old enough to do it myself.* But part of independence is knowing when you need support. Even adults ask others for help!

Expect imperfection. Know that at times things will not go as planned. We can't always predict what might happen. You set your intention, put in the effort…and then when something goes off track, take a breath, say some encouraging words to yourself, and try again.

And forget perfection. Perfection is impossible, obviously. If we expect ourselves to be perfect, eventually we'll burn out. Stick to small steps, one at a time, and give yourself a pat on the back each time you succeed. And when you forget something and lose track, that's fine too—the most important moment is remembering to try again.

Many people experience uncertainty about new plans at the start. *I'm going to meditate every day at bedtime (but ha ha, not really).* It's natural to have doubts. Maybe your inner critic again chimes in, "Yeah, whatever, you'll try, but you'll never remember to meditate. You always forget." Notice that those thoughts really exist but are not necessarily true. You won't know what works for you until you give it an actual try.

Because mindfulness can directly help with focus, emotional self-control, and other aspects of ADHD, start with a plan. If mindfulness becomes a habit, you will face your other challenges more easily. You might see things like staying on top of assignments and struggles with planning get easier, while procrastinating less. As we mentioned in chapter 1, mindfulness won't rid you of ADHD, but it puts you behind the steering wheel rather than ADHD leading the way.

Creating a Mindfulness Habit

Now that we know that mindfulness can be as simple as listening with attention to music, you can start with that habit. Use the outline we just reviewed:

Create a specific plan using small steps. We suggest one goal to start: music meditation every day for five to ten minutes (which again, is fun and easy). For every practice you list, specify the *time* you'll do it and the *place* you'll do it, for example:

Music meditation

Time I will do it: 9:30 p.m., before bed

Place I will do it: in my bedroom

Above all, be compassionate with yourself. Would you expect a friend to get everything right the first time? Of course not. Throughout this process of developing a mindfulness habit, you don't have to be perfect. Do your best and let go of the rest.

Connect new habits to old and be specific. Pick something you already do regularly and tie your mindful music practice to it. For example, you already brush your teeth before bed. Spend five minutes doing music meditation right after you brush your teeth.

Set up reminders. Set an alarm for when you'll do your music meditation each day. You can even make it musical! When you hear that alarm, remind yourself that this is a time to simply listen to music you like—without having to do anything else.

If you tie music meditation to brushing your teeth, you might put a sticker on the bathroom mirror that says "music" or draw musical notes on your toothbrush.

Whatever reminder you use, write it down in your mindfulness habit plan, as you wrote down the time and place:

Reminders I will create: an alarm on my phone; a sticky note on my bedside table

Reward yourself. After your music meditation, do something nice for yourself. This can be anything you enjoy. At least, say something kind to yourself like, *You're awesome! You stuck to your new routine! That's not easy!*

Partner with someone. It's harder to forget and to make excuses if someone else is involved with your plan. It's not always possible, but wherever you can, see if a friend or an adult can help you remember. Maybe both you and a friend can do your music meditation at the same time, for example.

Most of all, be kind to yourself if you miss a practice. Simply start again the next day. *Music meditation, every day after brushing my teeth. Right, forgot it totally yesterday. But tonight, here I am, starting over.*

I started to practice mindfulness because my life was a mess. I was eating Cheetos and Red Bull for breakfast, and I never took notes in class, and of course never did homework. I was failing four out of my five classes and felt like crap. Our school counselor talked to my health class about mindfulness, and I thought I'd give it a try. I mean, why not, nothing to lose. The counselor said to do it at the same time every day, right after I do something I always do. So I listened to music after my Cheetos. I put a sign on the snack shelf that said MUSIC so I would remember. And it worked—I really listened to the music. Did nothing else. It was super relaxing not to have to worry about anything during that time and just listen. And I felt so good afterward that I didn't feel like I needed a reward—but I took an extra bag of Cheetos with me to school anyway—figured I deserved it!

—Juan, age 17

For the next few weeks, do your best with this plan. What counts is your effort and being kind to yourself in the process. Here's a big tip that will help: much of the struggle starting a new plan comes from not fully committing.

Often, we say we'll do something but don't believe it's all that likely, or valuable. A new plan is harder to follow when you are not really sure whether you want to bother with it. You say you will one day, back off the next, change your mind the third, and on and on. When you seriously commit to your plan, it gets a whole lot easier.

Check in with how your practice is going too. Are you making mindfulness easy? Remember, it is time for yourself. It can be fun and easy, expecting nothing of you other than, say, listening to your music. It is about taking care of yourself.

If you mess up and forget? Notice if you feel angry with yourself and your inner critic acts up. When you find yourself beating yourself up, remember your practice. See if you can say instead, *Whoops! I forgot. I'm human and everyone forgets sometimes. I'll do better tomorrow.* We all have false starts with new habits.

The most important moment when we lose touch with our intentions is when we notice and come back again. Without giving yourself a hard time, start over. Check your reminder alarms, and make an extra effort to do your music meditation the next day. Later, when you are ready, add another practice or try a different practice.

Regular mindfulness practice helps you remember the informal practices when you need them. Those practices—like Soles of the Feet or Three Mindful Breaths—can be done right in the moment you're feeling upset. Obviously, you can't set reminders or designate a time for those. You don't know when the need will come up! Stick to your formal mindfulness habit for a while, and you'll see—mindfulness, both formal and informal, will become part of your life.

Summing It Up

Our lives are driven by habits. Habits about how we think about ourselves. Habits about how we think about challenges. Habits about how we talk to people and our health and so many other ways that we live. Taking control of our lives starts with seeing the habits we want to change and deciding to change them.

Being mindful helps us be aware of one particularly difficult habit: listening to our hypercritical inner voice. It's a part of us that isn't usually speaking the truth. When we're more mindful, we hear that voice clearly and make a conscious choice about whether we want to believe it. *Thanks anyway, I'm doing everything I can.* Letting go of self-criticism helps us take charge of our lives.

In the next chapter, you'll learn about how ADHD affects communication, a particularly stressful part of ADHD for many people. You'll see how to cut down on ADHD taking over and dominating conversations, and how mindfulness and self-compassion make that easier.

CHAPTER 4

Making Yourself Heard: Mastering Communication

When a bunch of people are talking at once, it starts sounding like noise, like at a restaurant. The words get jumbled. I try to figure out when to talk, and then I interrupt someone. Or they get annoyed because they told me something and I missed it—my parents hate that the most. I'm trying, but it still happens a lot, and when I feel anxious it makes everything worse. But you know what's great? Sometimes now I secretly massage one hand with the other under the table, and feel a little better. I'm not sure what it does, but it works.

—Leona, age 18

Let's face it, conversation can be hard. Your ADHD can get you distracted or make you interrupt people. Difficulties with executive function might make keeping up with fast conversations difficult. Or you might lose track of details that are important. Staying patient when you have something burning inside you that you want to say isn't easy either. In the end, to communicate well and build friendships, you'll want to be aware of how ADHD affects everyday conversation.

Here, too, being mindful can help. With mindfulness, we stay more aware of what's actually going on in any moment. In a conversation, that may be as simple as having the awareness and compassion for yourself to confidently tell a friend, "I'm too distracted right now to have a serious talk on the bus. Can we connect again later?" Standing up for yourself in this way is an act of self-compassion.

In this chapter, we'll look at common ways ADHD impacts communicating. Then we'll explore mindful and compassionate conversational skills that will change your experience for the better.

The Impact of ADHD on Communication

Whether you want your parents to let you stay out late or to ask a classmate to hang out, you have to be able to communicate. If we ultimately want someone to listen to us, how we stand, our tone, and the words we select all influence the likelihood that will happen.

Of course, as you learned in chapter 1, your brain manager may not always be doing its job fully. You may get flustered by someone, and anxiety takes over. Or other emotions muddle your thinking, and you can't figure out how to express yourself. And then, how you act when you're emotionally charged changes how people respond to you; maybe you say something snarky by accident. Before you know it, the words "You're so annoying!" come tumbling out of your mouth.

Some ADHD symptoms can end up affecting people around you—for example, being overly talkative, interrupting, and impulsive. Some symptoms are more internal, since keeping track of information you're hearing, focusing on the speaker, and organizing what to say all rely on executive function. Either way, change always starts with awareness. If ADHD affects how you communicate, seeing that accurately is the first step in doing something about it.

What's more, no one is a perfect communicator. We all benefit from working on staying settled and listening clearly. Expressing ourselves gets difficult from time to time...or a lot of the time even.

What is Leona, from the start of this chapter, experiencing? Well, for one thing, it's her ADHD. But more than that, she's working on listening and taking her turn. And as a huge first step, she's learning to be compassionate with herself. That lets her stay settled long enough to either listen better or ask for a break.

As you can see, being mindful can help us connect with others and get our needs met. We stick to our intentions because we feel more balanced, stay calmer (*I'm not sure I got my point across yet, but I better wait my turn*), and avoid self-criticism (*I think I misspoke, but it's okay. I'll go back and try again*). It's all good news: you can train yourself to communicate better.

Communicating Mindfully

Steering a conversation effectively relies on your self-awareness. That means recognizing what to say and when, and how it may come across to others. In the end, the way *we* think and act are the only things under our control in any situation.

Of course, it's impossible to stay aware all the time. It's a lot to keep track of what you're thinking, what comes out of your mouth, and others' reactions too. That's especially true when a lot is going on around you. Distracted, you might say something off topic or lose track of who's

63

talking. But then, any moment you *become* aware allows you to guide the conversation more skillfully again.

Which aspects of communication are hardest for you? What do you struggle with most?

- Blurting out when someone else is speaking

- Talking too much, or over other people

- Listening closely

- Getting your thoughts organized quickly, so that others follow what you're saying

We're here to help you with all these struggles, using self-awareness and self-compassion. Let's explore first what to do before speaking, then during speaking, and then after speaking.

Before Speaking: Staying Ahead of Your ADHD

Notice your emotional state. Emotions can feel all-consuming and cloud our thinking. Is it possible to have a reasonable conversation right now? Can you calm yourself before continuing, or ask for a break? Sometimes the most skillful path is to politely ask to step away for a bit. But what if someone is asking to talk now, and you can't put it off? If you're feeling frenzied, jittery, or angry, and you *have* to have a conversation, here are a few things you can try before you start:

- Take three mindful breaths.

- Feel the sensation of your feet on the floor, grounding yourself. Stay with this for at least ten seconds.

- Pay attention to sounds. (You'll read more about this later in this chapter.)

If you have time, organize your thoughts. For an important conversation, jot down a few notes of what you want to say, and lay out your reasoning. *Mom, Dad, this is why I think I should be able to go away with my friends this weekend.* Once the conversation starts, you may feel anxious or it may take a wrong turn; if you have your bullet points nearby, you can turn to them for a reminder of what to say.

While Speaking: Learning how to Communicate with Strength and Skill

First, listen closely. Being a good listener is one quality of a good friend. Other people like to be listened to. That doesn't mean only staying silent but does mean trying to attend to every word they say, like you did earlier with a piece of music. It is often useful, even if you disagree overall, to find a point of agreement to start. *Mom, Dad, I know we all want me to be safe, and to be happy.*

Notice how you carry your body, including your facial expression. We're not always aware of what we're expressing with our bodies. If you're frowning, staring at your phone, have your arms crossed, or seem aggressive in how you stand, that says something to others. You can give an impression of not caring even when you're trying to be supportive. Notice your body and adjust your stance to show that you're interested.

Notice your thoughts. Sometimes during conversation, we create stories in our heads about where someone else is taking the conversation. Are you making assumptions about the intentions of the speaker, or guessing what they will say next? Are your thoughts drifting, as thoughts do, into past or future worries?

We might, for example, get defensive, assuming we're in trouble because in the past we've been blamed a lot. Right then, we don't realize that someone was about to compliment us instead. When you find yourself jumping into the future, come back to what's actually being said—like in your music practice.

Speak with intention. Pause before you speak and consider your words. Practice taking a few breaths before saying anything. Ask yourself these three questions before starting:

Is it true?

Is it kind?

Is it necessary?

Stay honest with yourself! If the answer isn't yes to all three questions, it's probably best not to speak. The same concept, by the way, holds true for texting and social media postings. To paraphrase an old saying, before speaking or messaging, make certain your words are an improvement over the silence.

FORMAL PRACTICE: **Listening to Sounds All Around You**

Now, let's try another short mindfulness practice that will help build communication skills—specifically, listening carefully. Because it involves sounds, not words yet, it is particularly fun outside in nature. But it doesn't have to be done that way—indoor sounds are cool also. You can do this practice anywhere.

Find a place where you can stretch out and be comfortable. Maybe in your backyard on the grass, or sitting on a bench, or even near a window where you can hear both inside and outside sounds.

Then decide how long to spend on this practice. It might be five minutes, but you can start with fewer if you want. Set a timer on your phone that is a gentle ring—you don't want to be jarred out of this practice. This practice is easier with your eyes closed. That limits visual distractions.

If you'd like, close your eyes.

Now bring your attention to sounds around you.

Simply notice sounds. Play around with noticing sounds far away, sounds closer in, and even ones that are right next to you. That's the only thing you have to do—listen to sounds.

You may notice thoughts come up. *That's the ice cream truck, wait, if I don't get out soon it will drive away and...*When that happens, acknowledge those thoughts by silently saying the word "thinking" to yourself. Do this with each thought, and then let the thought drift away. Then return to listening to sounds.

If a sound exists that is unpleasant, notice that too.

It's all part of what is happening right now. Notice what you're feeling when you hear an unpleasant sound. Then return to listening.

When the alarm rings, gently open your eyes if they've been closed.

Try to extend this practice from time to time. If you start with five minutes, when you're up for it, extend to seven minutes. Don't overdo it. Really listening for a few minutes is better than a longer time not really listening.

Besides being pleasant, listening to sounds strengthens listening in general. It gets easier to notice when our mind wanders and to come back. Once we get better with sounds, it becomes easier to focus on someone's voice. And voila, conversation becomes easier!

After Speaking: The Art of Communication Repair

Up to this point, we've discussed when communication more or less goes well. Sometimes, you'll have conversations that get off track. You're doing your best to really listen to your parent, maybe, and then they push you too far. Your frustration builds and you lose it. You yell at them and storm out of the room. What next?

Enter: Communication repair. Part of being a good communicator includes admitting when you didn't get your thoughts across well and trying again. Repair means figuring out what went wrong and doing what's necessary to fix it. Sometimes it means apologizing for your role in the breakdown. Remember, none of us gets everything right all the time. You *will* have moments when your ADHD drives you to say something not so great. And there *is* a process for fixing that. Let's look at it now.

After a conversation, pause and give yourself a little compassion. Check in with yourself. In this moment, you probably feel a little bad, or a lot, and can use self-compassion. If your inner critic is screaming out, "You totally blew it and they all hate you now," remember you are human, and all humans make mistakes.

Notice that self-critical voice and remember you don't have to believe it. Once again, say whatever you might to a good friend. Maybe something like, *Wow, this is really hard right now. I'm so sorry you have to go through this!*

Use your mindfulness practice. Miscommunicating is stressful, but figuring out what to do next is easier once you calm down. Mindfulness practices cool you off if you get heated and upset. Take a few mindful breaths or focus on the soles of your feet on the floor. (See the exercise in chapter 1.) Remember, mindfulness is purposeful. Once you settle, you can see better what to do next.

Take a moment to consider what happened. See if you can sort out what went wrong. Is there something that you need to clarify? Would writing a few notes for yourself before restarting the conversation help? Is there something more to learn or ask about? Do you want to seek advice from someone you trust?

Set up a time to try again. Once you have an idea of what is needed, set up a time to make it happen. Whatever happens in the conversation, aim to stay aware without judging yourself. In other words, you might say, "I didn't mean to scream and run out of the room, but you weren't listening to me!" And then realize that maybe you shouldn't have added the "you weren't listening to me" part. Don't beat yourself up about it. Do a "repair within the repair" and say something like, "but I know you were trying to listen."

We can give ourselves permission to make mistakes when communicating. Perhaps you didn't get your point across and need another time to talk or write a note. Apologizing itself is a sign of strength, not weakness. All these follow-up steps are part of effective communication.

The key is realizing when you run into problems in conversation, as you inevitably will, and to keep practicing. If you struggle with communication repair, that's okay too. This is a lifelong practice that many adults continually work on.

Another option to calm yourself down is to consider supportive touch—like in the practice that comes next.

INFORMAL PRACTICE: **Supportive Touch**[10]

Right in the middle of a tough conversation, without anyone knowing, you can settle yourself. Here's an easy and quick way to try when something makes you feel uneasy, alone, or angry. As we've mentioned, because it's done right when you need it, it's called an informal practice.

When we want to soothe our dog or cat, we pet them, right? Or maybe we put them on our laps. This feels good for the dog or cat—the dog may close its eyes and roll over for a belly rub, or the cat will purr. Our natural instinct to soothe others provides three things: soft words, gentle touch, and physical warmth. When a toddler tries to walk, falls, and cries, an adult might pick them up, say something soothing, and rub their back, providing those same three things: soothing words, gentle touch, and physical warmth.

Research suggests these three activities promote a release of oxytocin in our bodies—our "feel good" hormone.[11] That makes our pets feel good, and toddlers too. And of course, physical comfort from others—a hug or a pat on the back—makes us feel good too.

We don't usually soothe *ourselves* this way, but we can. Why not? When something upsets you—like you've interrupted a conversation or said something off topic, and get strange looks, try one of these supportive touches:

Hold one hand in the other and rub the back of one hand with your thumb.

Rest your hand over your heart and feel the light pressure and warmth of your hand.

Cross your arms and rub both upper arms with your hands.

Gently massage your face or your forehead with one or both hands.

Remember, you are human. All humans mess up and make mistakes. When you're embarrassed or angry at yourself, take a moment to settle.

If supportive touch feels a little strange, it's likely because you're not used to it. Think about the first time you played a music solo or cooked a complicated recipe; it probably felt awkward. If you get into the habit of using supportive touch, you'll soon feel comfortable with it. A lot of teens like simply putting a hand over their heart. They say it makes them feel safe and protected.

If you don't feel comfortable with supportive touch, that's okay too. You can try noticing that it feels uncomfortable and do it anyway, to see what that's like.

Another option you can try, if you don't want to do supportive touch, is to take a moment to say something kind to yourself like you might for a friend. For a few breaths, notice fully what you are experiencing as you breathe in. *Wow, I'm freaking out.* And then on each out-breath, gently wish yourself well: *I wish to stay strong and kind to myself right now.* In an unforced way, remind yourself of what you most wish for and repeat that to yourself. In with awareness, and out setting an intention.

Summing It Up

Communicating skillfully is an art that develops with practice. When you're aware and settled, handling your internal world (like your emotions) and your external world (like how you talk to your friends) is easier. That then affects how people treat you back. You may feel less frustrated and get along with others more easily.

Skillful communication also involves knowing what to do when you *aren't* able to communicate well, like when anger or impatience intrude, as they do sometimes. You've now learned how to do that too.

Mindfulness and self-compassion practice support communication skills so you can get your point across effectively without hurting others' feelings or getting yourself hurt. Staying compassionate with yourself affects your relationship with people around you for the better too. And speaking of feelings, the next chapter gives you tools for staying balanced at times when feelings become overwhelming.

CHAPTER 5

Staying Calm While Dealing with Emotions

One time, one of my best friends, he said he had to stop playing online games with me. He couldn't handle how angry I got—it stressed him out. All at once, I realized no way could I bother a friend so much by acting like that.

—Henry, age 13

Having issues with regulating your emotions is commonly part of ADHD. That can mean being quick to get angry or frustrated, or feeling like giving up when things get hard. ADHD can amplify your anxiety. That's because your brain manager is responsible for noticing emotions without overreacting. Around half of people with ADHD get easily triggered;[12] emotions show up and they feel like they're drowning in those feelings.

But you can learn to "surf" these feelings instead.

Our emotions are simply energy states, coming and going throughout our bodies. They may feel permanent, but they always change. When we're aware of them, we can surf them like waves, letting them come and go. When we're not aware of them, they can take on a life of their own.

How Emotions Affect Us

Emotions influence how we act and get along. When we're caught up in stress or anxiety (*I can't believe she's talking to me that way...*), emotions can change our thinking. Because stress can cause us to shut down mentally, we may find ourselves at a loss for words. Or unable to think clearly on a test. Or totally missing a goal in soccer.

If we ignore or fight against difficult feelings, they get worse. We make difficult situations *more* difficult because bottling up painful emotions actually makes them grow in intensity.

> I wanted to hang out with Tyra outside of school for months. She said no, no matter what I came up with. Then I decided, whatever, and started ignoring her. I'd walk away if I saw her. It felt better for a while to pretend I didn't care. But I was hurt. And angry. And down on myself too, like why didn't she like me? I was a mess and acted like a dope.
>
> —Pablo, age 16

When you fight or avoid an emotion, it usually backfires. You're not only sad, you're also angry about being sad. Or you're sad and have eaten too many cookies trying to make yourself happy, and now you're sad, nauseated, and annoyed with yourself. Maybe you yell at a friend and push them away. We complicate emotions when we get caught up in them mindlessly.

On the other hand, practicing mindfulness and self-compassion provides you with new and healthier ways to deal with strong emotions. It becomes a whole lot easier to create a space to *first* notice emotions and *then* figure out how to respond. With an unpleasant emotion, it is easy to go off as those feelings explode. And yet, even when something feels bad, it's useful to stay intentional about how we manage it. When we do, we respond in a way that's effective for us and beneficial in the long run.

The practice in the next section builds this skill of responding effectively when emotions surge.

Taking the Wheel Back from Our Emotions

I'm not sure how to explain, but it's like, now when I start getting anxious, I breathe a little while. Then I can think clearly again.

—Sam, age 15

It's not so easy to experience emotions, either fun ones or not-so-fun ones, without getting swept away. It takes a strong brain manager to experience intensity without immediately reacting to it. Thankfully, mindfulness and self-compassion directly build this ability, even when our brain manager seemingly has been sleeping on the job. Research has repeatedly shown that both mindfulness and self-compassion help directly with stress and emotion.

Our experiences without mindfulness often look like this:

Something happens.

We feel an emotion
(for example, anger, sadness, boredom, frustration).

We react.

With mindfulness, they look like this:

Something happens.

We pause. We allow ourselves to feel whatever we feel.
We don't fight these feelings, try to escape, or push them away.
We notice the feelings in our body. When we notice a story line
going on in our heads about why we're angry, we aim to let
that story go. We come back again to feelings in our body.

We decide how to respond.

We respond.

It's not easy to recognize feelings right as we experience them. But with practice, you observe emotions and name them. Research has shown that identifying an emotion makes it less powerful.[13] One expression for this is: *name it and you tame it.*

When we feel an emotion, we experience sensations in our bodies. That's the next step: recognizing what happens physically when the emotion comes up. What sensations do you feel? Tension, tightening, or maybe even physical pain? Maybe you feel guilt in your belly, or stress tightness in your face. An expression for this is: *feel it and you heal it.*

In addition to awareness of our feelings, we can practice self-compassion: We soften the tense place in our body. We imagine relaxing it a bit. We soothe ourselves with comforting words or thoughts. We remain open to our emotions by allowing them to stay, instead of running away or lashing out at them. We see them and give them room, because we can't force them away anyway. This last part is called *soften, soothe, allow.*

We can put this all together into an exercise that uses these three steps—*name it to tame it, feel it to heal it,* and *soften, soothe, allow*—to respond to difficult emotions we all feel in a way that's effective, not reactive.

FORMAL PRACTICE: **Working with Difficult Emotions**[14]

This practice asks you to think of a difficult situation you're dealing with and then to practice using three steps to surf them more easily. In real life, you can do it right when difficult emotions come up. At https://www.newharbinger .com/46394, you'll find an audio recording of the practice.

Find a comfortable position. Close your eyes and take three relaxing breaths. If you'd like, stroke your arms, put your hand on your heart, or use another support-ive gesture. Remind yourself that you are human and that you deserve kindness.

Picture a challenging situation. Let yourself recall a mild to moderately diffi-cult situation in your life right now. Maybe you had a difficult conversation with someone. Maybe you had a problem with a friend or parent, or in school. Maybe something happened that left you feeling left out and unappreciated. Visualize the situation. Who was there? What was said? What happened? Try to get a good image of it in your mind.

Avoid choosing either your most difficult problem or a tiny one. Choose one that generates a little stress in your body when you think about it, without over-whelming you.

Name it to tame it. Start by labeling your emotions. See if you can name the different emotions you experience while thinking about the situation. This list includes some common emotions:[15]

Anger (frustrated, annoyed, jealous, furious)

Sadness (lonely, grieving, heartbroken, depressed)

Fear (insecure, anxious, vulnerable, sad)

Disgusted (reluctant, resistant, bored, uninterested)

Joyful (happy, excited, appreciative, delighted)

Loving (affectionate, connected, compassionate, caring)

If you notice several emotions, name the strongest one for this exercise. If two or more emotions tie for first place, choose one for now.

Repeat the name of the emotion to yourself in a gentle, understanding voice: *This is fear,* or *This is loneliness.* Simply name the emotion as if you were a scientist observing it.

When you're naming your emotion, use the same warmhearted tone of voice that you would use with a friend. If you said to your friend, "Wow, you're really feeling sad," what tone of voice would you use?

Feel it to heal it. Now expand your awareness of the emotion to your body as a whole. Recall the difficult situation and scan your body for where you physically feel that strong emotion. In your mind, move your awareness slowly from your head to your toes, pausing where you sense tension or discomfort.

Now choose a single location where the feeling seems strongest. Perhaps you notice a tense, achy muscle, or heartache, or tightness in your stomach, chest, or throat. Recognize how this emotion feels in your body right now.

Soften, soothe, allow. Now see if you can soften the area in your body where you feel the sensation. Let that part of you relax as if applying heat to sore muscles. You can say quietly to yourself, *Soft...soft* or *Let go, let go,* or any words that make sense to you.

Remember, you are not trying to force the sensation away. Hold the sensation delicately, like you might a lightning bug you caught. See if you can pay attention to the emotion without wrestling with it for a moment.

Note that emotions may sometimes feel too big to work with at first. In that case, simply naming your emotion is helpful. So is staying with the sensations you notice in your body. If you want to only acknowledge the sensations you find, stay with that part of the practice for now.

If you feel ready, once you've softened where your body feels the emotion most, soothe yourself. Offer yourself care because you are struggling with a strong emotion. You could put your hand over your heart and feel your body breathe. Or focus on supportive words, like *This is really hard.* Or acknowledge you're feeling an emotion everyone feels: *I know I'm not the only person who has ever felt this way* or *Other teens feel this way too.*

Can you let go of the wish for the emotion to disappear? Let this strong emotion stay without trying to fix or change it. This is the aim—allow whatever feelings are here to be here and let go of fighting them a bit. With that, maybe you can watch the emotion slowly melt away.

These three words, "Soften...soothe...allow," are ones you can repeat, like a favorite saying, as a reminder to offer yourself a little kindness and warmth in moments of difficulty or when you're struggling.

Slowly open your eyes when you're ready.

To summarize, you've worked on three skills:

- Labeling emotions—"Name it and you tame it."

- Mindfulness of emotions in your body—"Feel it and you heal it."

- Opening to your emotions and gently making space for them— "Soften, soothe, allow."

With practice, your emotions may get a little lighter or less intense. We wouldn't expect a dramatic shift with one practice, but maybe, as time goes on, you'll notice a lessening of any emotional heaviness.

Here we wrote out all the steps for you in a formal way, with a difficult situation from the past. But you can do this practice quickly, even in the middle of a tough conversation. It can be an in-the-moment reminder to take care of your emotional experience.

Maybe someone says something to you that was really unfair. You're mad. You say to yourself something like, *Anger. This is anger.* You notice how that feels like a weight on your chest. You can see emotions without engaging in old patterns like ignoring or lashing out (*I'm pissed off so I'm going to go yell at my sister!*).

This approach to managing emotions is proven and practical. In fact, awareness of emotions in their bodies is one way athletes and other people who need to stay calm under pressure manage stress. They may notice a rising heart rate first. Then they settle down *before* that feeling takes over and makes them miss the winning catch.

Seeing our emotions and allowing them to be there, while taking care of ourselves in the moment, gives us the space to choose how we want to respond and the ability to do it. Whatever we have to manage, we're responding rather than reacting out of habit.

As Pablo experienced:

My chest literally ached. And I kind of let that ache alone. Sure, it hurt, but at least I wasn't ignoring it. I imagined it melting. And I said to myself, "Hey, dude, it'll be okay. She's not the only one for you." I did that every day for a week! One day I realized I wasn't upset with Tyra anymore. We even chatted in the hall and it didn't feel so bad. And then, Lara asked me out to a movie, and we've been hanging out ever since.

Managing our emotions helps us feel better, but life isn't only about us. When you practice mindfulness and self-compassion, you'll feel steady and be less reactive around other people too. For example, someone says something you find offensive. Rather than lashing out, you catch yourself, label the emotion (*I'm pissed; that was insulting*), release the tension where you find it in your body (*I'm noticing the tightness in my shoulders softening*), and make a real choice in how to respond (*I'm walking away*).

That is not only a skillful way of handling a hard moment in time, but it probably improves how people treat you back. So the next time you start to feel a little, or a lot, emotional, sit down. Take a few breaths, and name what you're feeling. Then find the sensation it causes in your body, and practice soften, soothe, allow. You can't force emotions away, but you can learn to handle them with skill and ease.

Summing It Up

In this chapter, you learned how to mindfully observe your emotions, and you began exploring how to shift your emotional reactions. Handling emotions well doesn't mean you are okay with whatever happens. You're never pretending an unpleasant emotion feels good. But you make life easier by feeling your emotions rather than fighting with or hiding from them.

Stay patient while working with your emotions. Mindfulness and self-compassion plant seeds that will blossom in the future. No need to stress if nothing happens at first. If you watered a wilting plant, would you expect it to immediately sprout flowers? If you buried a seed today, would you expect a tree tomorrow?

Roots slowly develop once we plant a seed. But over time, seedlings form, and then with repeated watering and sunlight, we see growth. That same thing applies to you. Practice will help you deal better with your emotions, so that you'll surf the waves of these emotions and perhaps more often enjoy that ride.

In the next chapter, you'll see how managing your ADHD effectively is critical when it comes to your relationships with friends and family. So turn the page...

CHAPTER 6

Navigating a Complicated Social World

I loved Little League baseball, but it was hard for me because I'm not very good. I tried to get better, but I still always missed the ball when it mattered most. Or I'd be looking the other way. It got to the point where some guys didn't even want me on their team. But I loved it so much, I kept going back. And when we won, that feeling of being part of a team was awesome! And I still love sports. Going to games with my friends is the best.

—Maurice, age 17

With or without ADHD, teen relationships can be challenging. So let's look at how mindfulness and self-compassion allow you to navigate the shifting sands of your family relationships and social world.

Your friends are a central part of your life. ADHD can impact friendships in many ways. You may act impulsively. You may not plan ahead and suddenly Friday arrives, and everyone is out with someone else. You may get distracted right when your friend is telling you about this fascinating new classmate, and later realize you have no idea what they said. Maintaining relationships may be more difficult for you than for your peers—for now.

Over time, mindfulness provides the steadiness to see what's happening and what to do. So often in life, it's not that you need to learn something more (although sometimes that is true, of course), but that you need to settle long enough to remember what you already know. Along with self-compassion, mindfulness supports your resilience, particularly when altering behaviors that may not be serving you. For example, when you forget to plan your weekend, you take a few breaths and remember your caring self: *Everyone forgets sometimes. I'm doing great, this is hard!* You change *how* your ADHD impacts your social life, rather than getting stuck in frustration and sadness, believing that nothing can be done.

Common Humanity—We're All in This Together!

Every once in a while, I look around the lunch-room and realize, wow, we're all graduating soon. Everyone will be going on to something else. No more school. Everyone must be struggling to figure out the next step. It's intense.

—Miriam, age 18

All of us feel like outsiders at times. Even when it doesn't seem so, everyone you know experiences confusion figuring out who they are and how they fit in. Like you, they navigate changing relationships with friends and family, and all the emotions that arise from that. We all struggle to get along with people, as well as with the instinct to judge ourselves and others in ways that aren't quite fair. The understanding that we all struggle in life, and that we all feel diffi-cult emotions at times—like anxiety, fear, loneliness, or anger—is called common humanity.

It may seem like no one else experiences difficult feelings. Or that no one wrestles like you do with figuring out what to do. It can be hard to tell what your parents, teachers, and friends all want from you. When we feel insecure, angry, or at a loss, often our inner critic says, "You're the only one who hasn't figured it out." And yet, everyone everywhere strug-gles to understand other people and to be understood—*everyone*. Quite literally, we're all in this together.

This common experience is easy to forget in the middle of a hard moment, like realizing you said something completely off topic and you feel like everyone is staring at you. You may fall into a sense of *I'm the only one*. And yet, if you catch yourself you can recall instead: *Everyone has moments like this. I'm not alone!* We're more similar and connected to everyone around us than it often feels at first.

Seeing When ADHD Symptoms Affect Others

So, how does ADHD affect *your* social life?

Maybe ADHD doesn't affect this part of your life much at all. But for many people with ADHD, it does. Maybe you say something acci-dentally that makes someone angry. Maybe it's endlessly frustrating for you keeping up when people chat together in a noisy group. Maybe you feel like you're misunderstood by peers when you get off topic in a conversation. To be at your best with your peers often requires getting a handle on this sometimes frustrating part of ADHD.

Here are a few ways to begin:

Practice mindfulness and self-compassion. You're probably not surprised to hear us say this. If you find that you're anxious or agitated in a social situation, use an in-the-moment exercise to ground yourself. Try Soles of the Feet or Three Mindful Breaths. Remind yourself that everyone feels awkward or messes up socially sometimes. We all experience nervousness, uneasiness, and insecurity when wanting connection. It's because we all want to be cared for and safe. It's only human.

Quiet your inner critic. Your inner critic may get loud when you are interested in being friends (or more than just friends) with someone. It can make you feel far more awkward and off base, and you worry you've said something weird. For most people, their inner critic then recites everything wrong with them and a million reasons why this person would rather be friends with someone else. Maybe your inner critic aims to protect you, so you won't get your hopes up. Remember, though, that your inner critic isn't being rational and may not be offering you anything helpful.

Ask other people about their interests and emotions. People love talking about themselves. Ask what they like doing. *Hey, it's almost the weekend. What are you doing for fun?* Check and see what they feel, whether it's an everyday situation or something more complicated, like if someone seems upset or needs to talk about something. *You seem a little down today. Do you want to talk?* They will probably appreciate your asking.

Begin to notice when ADHD symptoms get in your way. If you are able to recognize your ADHD symptoms taking over, like speaking impulsively over someone, try catching yourself and pausing for a breath. Then say something like, "Sorry I interrupted. Go ahead." As you read in chapter 4, missing pieces of conversation leads to misunderstandings. If you feel like you missed something, repeat back what you've heard and confirm it is accurate. Say something like, "I'm just checking…did you mean to say that?" Paying attention to your own ADHD in this way, you learn to manage it over time. It's not so simple to do this, but it gets easier.

Think about your ADHD treatment. Consider this: if you had asthma and were wheezing, would you use your inhaler? Of course, you would! It's no different with ADHD. If you're more distracted or impulsive than you'd like, talk to your parents or your doctor about trying medication for ADHD. Working with a psychologist or other mental health professional might be valuable too, because they may have new tools you can use to move forward in your social world.

I was on the bus sitting with Ricardo, and he was talking about the soccer game. It was hard to hear him with everyone shouting, and I got angry with myself, because I didn't want him to think I wasn't listening. And, well, I also wanted to tell him about my new video game. So I paid attention to the feelings of my feet on the floor of the bus. I kept concentrating on the floor vibrating, and then I remembered to ask him a question first about his game. I think he really appreciated that I was interested.

—Sam, age 16

Talking with Friends About ADHD

Good friends naturally accept your quirks, just as you accept them for their quirks—and their unique and interesting qualities. Acceptance, though, doesn't mean overlooking our flaws and mistakes. We are accountable for our actions and can work on making changes to our behavior when we see the need.

For example, ADHD makes some people run late or forget things they need to do. If that's true for you, you'll want to be honest and open with your friends. You could say something like, "Yep, I run late all the time. I understand that's a stress for you and I'm sorry. I'm working on it!" Or "I really truly meant to call last night, but I got distracted." And then of course, watch for what causes those situations and take steps to manage those ADHD symptoms.

Taking responsibility means not just seeing when our behavior affects someone else but also taking necessary steps to make amends. That doesn't mean we need to beat ourselves up for our mistakes though. Staying compassionate with ourselves lets us more easily apologize and makes it more possible to do something different next time.

We can learn to *believe* that we're not bad for unintentionally hurting someone's feelings or forgetting to meet them for lunch. We can say to ourselves, *Well, I messed up. I'm only human, and I have ADHD, and so this is a little harder for me. Next time I'll put a reminder on my phone!* Feeling confident and with a new plan, apologizing to them gets a whole lot easier.

You might assure them not to take your mistake personally. You didn't forget to call because you don't care, for example, but because you sometimes get distracted and forget. When possible, make sure they understand that these are ADHD symptoms, not a reflection on how you feel about them. Quite importantly, if anyone continues to make you feel bad or won't let go of your mistakes, it may be time to question the value of their friendship, or to have a serious talk with them.

When Social Situations Get Complicated

Here's a scenario: A group of kids starts goofing off, and then the jokes get edgy and someone gets picked on. And then…what do you do? Do you get caught up in the teasing or step in and tone it down?

Or imagine this: Someone shows up with beer to a party and offers you one. Everyone else starts drinking and the next thing you know, all your friends jump into a car and you're not sure the driver is sober. What do you do?

These are tough situations to figure out. It's useful to consider ahead of time how to respond, rather than in the midst of the excitement. Spur-of-the-moment decisions—particularly when you're nervous or insecure—often aren't your best. If you're an impulsive decision maker, prone to getting carried away in social situations, it is easy to succumb to peer pressure. Spontaneity is great. And yet, for something as important as drinking or sex, for example, creating clear boundaries for yourself ahead of time helps you stick to your own best intentions.

Clearly you can't anticipate every possible scenario that might arise, but here are some common ones:

- You're at a party with alcohol, and you're underage or feeling pressured to drink.

- Friends dare you to drive too fast or want you to get into a car with someone who doesn't seem like a safe driver.

- You're dating this great person, and one of you feels ready to have sex, but one doesn't. Or you both do but don't have protection.

- You're at a party where someone is drunk and kids are treating them badly.

- You're home alone and find yourself feeling super depressed.

Stay in touch with your clear-sighted self by considering ahead of time the choices you'll make:

- I will make the choice that is kindest and safest for me.

- I will make the choice that is kindest and safest for others.

- If I need to get out of a difficult or uncomfortable social situation, I'll make a plan with my parent on how to manage that and still save face with my peers.

Keeping these three guidelines in mind, how would you respond to each of the situations provided above?

We'd just had this totally intense discussion in class about sex and dating, and I realized, it doesn't have to be so complicated. We just have to make sure to always treat each other nicely.

—Sean, age 19

Social Media and Relationships

Technology is probably a big part of your social world, whether it's texting, gaming, or social media. There's nothing inherently good or bad about smartphones and social media. They are simply tools. The important thing is staying aware of your choices with technology and how they make you feel.

Social media sometimes feels great and connects us with friends. But let's face it, it doesn't always leave us feeling good. Sometimes it makes us edgy and down. Or even lonely. It easily sets off another round of debate with our inner critic about why we're not worthy enough. Like any other tool, social media is all about how you use it.

Let's try this exercise to explore how you relate to social media.

EXERCISE: Exploring Social Media[16]

Make sure that you have a pen and paper with you to do this exercise. You can download an audio recording of this exercise at https://www.newharbinger.com/46394.

> Begin by closing your eyes and taking a moment to check in. Feel the movement of your breath as it flows in and out of your body.
>
> How are you feeling right now? Please write down anything you notice. Maybe you're feeling jittery in your chest. Or maybe something different—maybe you notice your stomach relaxing as you breathe and a softness in your face muscles.

Now pull out your phone, and open your most-used social media app. Take a minute to scroll through, paying attention to how what you're seeing makes you feel.

Write down feelings that come up while you're scrolling. For example:

I feel inspired.

I feel angry or sad.

I feel like I'm not good enough.

I feel entertained.

I feel lonely.

Offer yourself compassion for feelings of distress or unworthiness that may have arisen, perhaps saying to yourself:

May I treat myself with kindness in this moment.

May I know that I am enough, just as I am.

What would I say to a dear friend who was feeling this way?

Now asking yourself, *How could I treat myself more compassionately around my social media usage?* Write down any ideas. Here are a few prompts to consider:

What types of users do you follow?

Do certain posts consistently bring up self-criticism or distress?

What uses of social media make you feel good, or connected?

How much time do you spend online during an average day?

Remember, what's important is self-compassion and self-care. That means having the courage to step away from your phone if you're feeling sad, angry, lonely, frustrated, or hurt. Practicing mindfulness helps you remember to pay attention to how you're feeling in the moment. It's your choice. You always have the power to decide whether to engage with social media or not.

Sometimes I think I'm addicted to my phone. I love reading what's going on with my friends and celebrities. I like seeing that celebs are real people too! But one time I had this super awful experience. I saw all my friends hanging out together at the park, and no one told me about it... I felt totally rejected. Felt like someone punched me in the gut. I stayed in my room and cried all night.

—Dia, age 13

We know from research that more time online tends to make teens feel worse, not better. It can even increase the risk of depression and anxiety—when we feel that we can never stack up against what we see people doing or wearing or saying online, our self-confidence and self-esteem erode. Social media grabs our attention and pulls us in, but it isn't always moving us toward happiness.

Unfortunately, the momentary lift we get through our social media fix is inherently unsustainable. We feel good for a moment, but that feeling passes quickly. It leaves us grasping for the next like, message, or bonus in a game. That cycle of craving another good feeling through another fleeting online reward keeps us pinned to our devices, striving for the next one. This might be why teens who spend more time on devices report feeling more isolated and depressed.[17]

We also know that people present their best selves on social media. They create a persona and may use filters and apps to look better. They usually post only something exciting to share, not their "down" moments. Yet strangely, while we're aware of this, we unconsciously compare ourselves to what we see and our lives fall short. Everyone else looks better, has more excitement, gets more likes, and has more fun than we do.

Wise use of technology connects us to people who make us feel stronger and at ease. In fact, personal, face-to-face relationships matter most over the long run. Use social media to bond with people you care about and who care about you, and you'll feel more connected and present in your life.

What are some basic guidelines to healthy, happy social media time?

As a bottom line, stay mindful while on social media. Always make sure you use technology instead of being used by it. Remember this: anything posted online could get accidentally or intentionally shared. Would you be okay if your grandmother or your whole school saw what you are about to post? Check in with your intentions too. Is what you are posting kind? Thoughtful? Helpful?

Stay in touch with your emotions while online. When your emotions are heightened, like feeling angry or hurt, it is best not to post anything; directly connect with a friend instead. Tempting as it is to pour out your emotions on social media, pause. You'll be glad that you waited.

Lastly, consider this in-the-moment phone practice. Remember the idea of connecting new habits to old ones? Each time a phone notification pops up, use it as a mindfulness reminder. Before touching your phone, take three mindful breaths. And resist hurrying them so that you can get to your phone faster! After the third slow breath, attend to your phone.

In the Family

I was driving with my mom, and I was wearing this great dress that would be messed up by the seat belt, so I skipped it. And we weren't going very far; I figured nothing would happen. But my mom got all angry, and she started yelling she'd never let me drive again if I didn't listen. I did, but we didn't talk all that day. But once I calmed down, you know, she was right. I'm a good driver, but I could have lost my license. Or gotten hurt, I guess.

—Chan, age 16

Parents have a responsibility to keep their children safe—even if those children are teens. Chan felt that she was a careful driver and at first couldn't see that her mother was genuinely concerned about her safety. These conflicts with parents may come up more when you have ADHD, because demonstrating that you're responsible is harder. When your brain manager isn't always on the ball, you may accidentally do things you didn't mean to do too often (for now).

Parents may have their own issues. They may be afraid that you'll hurt yourself, get into an accident, not graduate from high school, become an ax murderer, or whatever else they dream up. Some of these fears may be based in reality, and some may not. In either case, try to stay patient. Parents are imperfect human beings, like all of us, and deserving of kindness and compassion.

Some tips for dealing with parents:

When you can, find quality time with your parent. Having a foundation of positivity and connection with your parent helps you in the long run. Hopefully, even when you disagree, you can still find emotional connection and hear useful advice now and then. Of course, not everyone is close with their parents, but think about this: even if you don't feel all that close with your parent today, isn't it easier to negotiate your weekend plans when you're feeling connected with them?

Notice that how you communicate matters, even when you disagree. If you lash out at your parent (*I hate you, you're the worst*), does that encourage a rational response? It's more likely they will see things your way if you stay calm. Mindful communication goes a long way in any situation, especially with your parent.

Take advantage of having a parent. If you see places a parent can be useful, like maybe with organization, or reminders, ask for help. This doesn't mean that you aren't being independent. It means that you know how to care for yourself.

Of course, if you need some space from your parent, that's okay. File away these ideas, and come back to them when they seem useful for you.

You can also try using your self-compassion skills with your parent. The next practice will help you deal with anger or resentment that often comes up with parents, when they're keeping you from doing what you want, pestering you about chores or homework, or complaining you're not trying hard enough. Or simply when you feel misunderstood again.

FORMAL PRACTICE: **A Person Just Like Me**[18]

It's best to do this practice when you're not *too* annoyed at your parent or caregiver. If you're too angry, it can be pretty hard. Pick a time when you might be a little annoyed but open to any feelings you have. Try it out and see what happens!

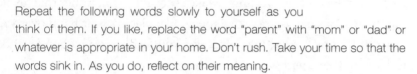

First, sit in a comfortable place and take a few deep, slow breaths. Allow yourself to feel the movement of your inhale and the movement of your exhale with each breath, taking your time.

Now bring an image of your parent or caregiver to mind. Think of them in as much detail as you can. For now, you can imagine them a safe distance away from you if you like.

Repeat the following words slowly to yourself as you think of them. If you like, replace the word "parent" with "mom" or "dad" or whatever is appropriate in your home. Don't rush. Take your time so that the words sink in. As you do, reflect on their meaning.

Consider a few things about your parent:

My parent is a human being, just like me.

My parent has a body and a mind, just like me.

My parent has feelings, emotions, and thoughts, just like me.

My parent has, at some point, been sad, disappointed, angry, hurt, or confused, just like me.

My parent wishes to be free from pain and unhappiness, just like me.

My parent wishes to be safe, healthy, and loved, just like me.

My parent wishes to be happy, just like me.

Now allow some wishes for this person to arise:

I wish for my parent to have the strength and support to help them through the difficult times.

I wish for my parent to be free from pain and suffering.

I wish for my parent to be strong and balanced.

I wish for my parent to be happy because they are human, just like me.

Take a few more deep breaths and notice what you're feeling.

When you're ready, gently open your eyes.

Were you surprised by anything that came up? There's no particular way you're supposed to feel. You may feel warm and fuzzy toward your parent or caregiver, or angry, or anywhere in between. You don't have to do anything with those feelings. Make space for them, rather than avoiding them. Consider a supportive touch, like placing your hand over your heart, if that feels soothing. Whatever you feel, see if you can let those feelings be there, without pushing them away.

Next time you find yourself getting heated with a parent or caregiver, take a mindfulness and self-compassion break. When your brain manager causes a misstep and you're feeling blamed for something out of your control, try to use your new communication skills (chapter 4) or your soften-soothe-allow practice (chapter 5). If you lose patience and lash out or behave in some way that doesn't reflect the kind of person you want to be, try out communication repair (chapter 4). We cannot choose our parents, but as with any relationship, we can always choose how we relate to them.

Summing It Up

Navigating social life in your teen years can be challenging. All too often, hurt feelings, anxiety, and stress abound. When your ADHD has gotten the best of you or you feel like you've said the wrong thing to someone, take a few minutes to remember that you are not alone. All teens struggle at times. At any given moment, teens everywhere feel just what you're feeling.

These difficult moments, even if they last weeks or months, won't last forever. You will move through them. Day to day, allow yourself space to mess up sometimes. Stay true to yourself, find connection when you're able, and your social world will come together to support you.

CHAPTER 7

Managing Time Before It Manages You

It keeps happening. I think I'm on top of things, and then Sunday comes and that "easy" project is so much bigger than I thought. It takes way longer to figure out what to do and then write it up. It's so frustrating, and then over and over, my parents get angry because I'm up late and I don't even know how I got there. And the pressure is through the roof! How did this happen again?

—Marita, age 14

A loud inner voice keeps telling you that it's fine to put things off, there's tons of time left. "No rush, dude, we'll get to it." If the task seems daunting, it seems even better to leave it to later. All of a sudden, you're stuck in that place again, with a way-bigger-than-you-expected project due in the morning. Your stress reaches an all-time high, and you don't know where to start.

Sound familiar? When your brain manager isn't up to speed, keeping up gets exhausting. Your body goes into fight-flight-freeze mode. You gear up to fight or to run away by releasing stress hormones, like cortisol and epinephrine. Your heart beats faster, and blood flows to your legs as you get ready to run. All of which is not so practical when you have to give a talk or finish a big assignment.

A little bit of stress is good. It gets you moving and motivates you. But *unrelenting* stress can be overwhelming. You want to scream at everyone in sight (fight), flee (run and hide) or freeze (ignore the assignment and hope no one notices). One way to understand freezing is this: When you're under attack, you don't want to waste time thinking, so rational thinking shuts down. Even though the kind of stressors we face now couldn't hurt us physically, our bodies don't know that.

That stress and anxiety are often worse with ADHD. You forget things and run behind, even when you care. *Oh shoot, was Mom's birthday yesterday?* It always feels hard to keep up, and that causes stress. On top of it, you may worry how that affects everyone around you, or that you're being judged by them. Research says nearly one-third of people with ADHD experience major levels of anxiety.[19] Your mindfulness practice is the perfect antidote to reduce that tension.

Mindfulness, a Brake for Anxiety

Any moment of practicing mindfulness is a moment managing anxiety. So much of anxiety happens because our thoughts get caught up somewhere else in time, in the past or future or spinning round and round a problem. Coming back by paying attention to any sensation in your body, even for a few moments, lets you leave anxious thoughts behind.

Each time you notice that your attention drifts into anxious thoughts, you can bring your attention back for a moment. You focus on a sensation in your body—feet on the floor, breath moving in and out of your body, or sounds nearby. That shift in focus drops you out of fight-flight-freeze mode and back in touch with what's actually going on. Sometimes you find whatever is happening isn't as anxiety provoking as your imagination. And if this *is* an anxiety-provoking moment, you may discover your thoughts are making it worse.

Much of our thinking is spent rehearsing fearful scenarios about the future (*What if I don't get that project done?*), rehashing the past (*That was so dumb of me to wait until the last minute to study for that test!*), or ruminating about a problem (*There just has to be a way to get these two papers done, go to the movies, and be home by curfew. I know there is!*). The 3 Rs—rehearsing, rehashing, and ruminating—consume our awareness for hours on end.

When we're mindful, we notice sooner when we're barreling into mental "time travel." We come back to what's in front of us, which otherwise may not get much attention at all. We recognize when thoughts make a challenging situation even more challenging. Differentiating between what we can feel and experience for real, right now, and racing, fearful thoughts is a critical step toward managing our lives well.

One day, I was practicing mindful breathing. Feeling my breath. Then thoughts came up, and all of a sudden it was like Star Wars, where they go into hyperdrive, and the stars zoom by. I realized, *I'm here, and those stars are my thoughts.* I came back to feeling my breath, and the stars slowed down. I kept doing that, and they moved more and more slowly. After a while, I didn't feel as worried about everything.

—Julian, age 17

Here is the deal with practicing mindfulness: you'll be distracted and restless, with or without ADHD. It gets easier, but there's no expectation of complete stillness. Sometimes it is relaxing and sometimes it isn't. And it's all fine. You're aiming to notice what you're feeling right when it happens and to strengthen skills that build resilience. Whatever happens is actually okay.

FORMAL PRACTICE: **Mindful Breathing**

Paying attention to your breath gives you an anchor for your attention. If you notice your mind wandering, simply bring your attention back to your breath moving in and out of your body. No need to judge yourself for getting distracted; it's normal. Less self-judgment means you're practicing both patience and self-compassion too. You can find an audio recording of this practice online at https://www.newharbinger.com/46394.

Set a timer for a short amount of time, like five or ten minutes.

Find yourself a comfortable posture. You can sit in a chair or on the floor. You can even lie down, if you don't think you'll fall asleep.

You can either lower your gaze toward the floor or close your eyes.

As you sit, start to notice that there is a physical movement in your body each time you take a breath. Feel that sensation of movement as best as you're able. There's nothing else to do. You're breathing, that's all.

With each breath, note in your mind, *breathing in…breathing out.* Let go of pushing for anything specific to happen. You're not trying to relax or be calm. You are just focusing on one breath at a time.

Almost immediately, your thoughts will go off somewhere else. That's not a problem. The most important moment is the one when you notice your mind has wandered. When that happens, simply guide your awareness back to your breath.

No need for self-criticism. It's common to think, *I'm not good at this, I'll never get it.* But you can't be good or bad at mindfulness, because you're not trying to stop your thoughts. When your mind wanders, that's part of the practice… you notice it's wandered, and you come back to feeling the next breath. Maybe remind yourself, *Great job, I'm back!*

As best as you're able, stay with the practice until the timer goes off. If you're distracted and lost in thought the whole time apart from one or two breaths, that's fine. That's what our minds do, but as we practice we get better at coming back more often. Whenever you notice your attention wandered and then came back—those are moments of mindfulness.

When the timer goes off, pause a moment. You may notice that you feel bored, or restless and edgy, wanting to move on. See if you can take just a moment to acknowledge that edginess and decide which moment to get up and move on with your day.

Once you're in a steadier place—not overwhelmed with anxiety—you can better address whatever is causing you to feel off-balance in the first place. With ADHD, that often relates to two common time management challenges we'll discuss next: time blindness, and…wait for it… procrastination.

Time Blindness

It's definitely helpful to schedule myself for forty minutes of work, and then a twenty-minute break. I can focus that long, and then it keeps my breaks on track too. As long as I study that way, I get the work done and I'm not nearly as distracted.

—Rebecca, age 20

People with ADHD frequently experience something called time blindness. It's far too hard keeping track of time, guessing how long things will take, and finishing activities that take a long time. You may lose track of time in the middle of a project, and then suddenly the whole afternoon passes. You may assume that a project will take an hour when it's more likely to take five. That means that you may not plan for enough time to complete the project, causing another intense Sunday night of schoolwork anxiety.

It's also difficult to proceed with a big project if you can't break it into smaller steps. If you had to bake a cake with no recipe, where would you begin? A recipe gives you careful notes about what to do in each step. Having a plan allows your stress level to drop considerably too. Seeing a logical way forward means that, even before you start, you'll feel better.

Later in this chapter we'll look at specific ways to handle larger projects. For now, let's look at a second obstacle to managing your time.

Procrastination

Your ADHD voice may say things like, "Don't bother doing that assignment now—you'll have plenty of time later!" That ADHD voice craves the easy, fun stuff before dealing with challenging tasks. Or maybe, you don't even remember to get started at all until something jars your memory—*Paper is due!*—and you rush into crisis mode. Those tasks involve your asleep-at-the-wheel brain manager, who either loses track or doesn't want to deal with the effort—or both. With ADHD, it may feel like managing time is completely out of your control.

Tackling procrastination is more complicated than deciding to start sooner. Some common reasons for procrastination are:

Avoiding things that are too hard. Tasks that takes extra mental effort may feel overwhelming when you have ADHD. When effort feels uncomfortable, you might get anxious and never start.

Productive distraction. Productive distraction means seeking out less burdensome tasks while avoiding something unpleasant. Maybe you convince yourself it's finally time for your chores instead of reading a chapter in your chemistry book, even though your homework is due tomorrow. But really, emptying the dishwasher is a whole lot more palatable right now than a dense science text.

Inaccurate time estimation. Because you underestimate how long something takes, you may put off doing it. Which wouldn't be bad if the task actually took just twenty minutes. Leaving it seems to make sense. Then you're stuck with Sunday night anxiety when you realize it will take a couple of hours, not twenty minutes after all.

Actual procrastination. And then of course, sometimes it's simply procrastination. You put things off until you absolutely cannot wait any longer. It's another ADHD trap, because it gets easier to focus when you're panicked. You focus better, but then your work is rushed, unedited, and not your best.

Consider giving that voice of procrastination a name, to reinforce that it's only one part of you, and not one you *have* to listen to. You may say to yourself, *I still have the rest of the weekend. One more episode.* Catching yourself, you reply, *Thanks, Pete the Procrastinator, for your suggestion, but time to stop watching now.* Practice recognizing thoughts that feel natural and easy but are actually Pete the Procrastinator mouthing off.

One start to countering that ADHD-related trait is noticing that Pete is not your wisest long-term advisor. He's all about doing what feels good now, rather than in the long run. Say something back to him, like, *Pete, you're not helping, so I'm not listening to you.* Then set up a firm plan to finish your homework first and then watch that episode.

Seeing a habit is the first step to changing that habit. Note the urge to delay and remind yourself that your future self—the one that later today has too much work to do—deserves better. Stay kind with yourself as you decide on a plan to achieve your goal. Habits are hard to change, and yours may not budge for a while. But by using what you've learned about mindful awareness (seeing ADHD clearly), self-compassion (treating yourself as you would a close friend having a hard time in school), and practical ADHD solutions (taking concrete steps to overcome difficulties with executive function), you can get on top of your time.

Deciding Where You're Going
Before You Set Out

A general desire to change behaviors is great but isn't a plan. Swearing to yourself you'll act differently tomorrow is a worthy thought but isn't a plan. Be specific with yourself while planning, and practice patience and self-compassion. In this way, *Be Patient with a Plan* can be a motto.

Try out the following approach, sometimes called planning backward. A general planning worksheet is available at https://www.newharbinger.com/46394 to use as well.

Picture your end point. Write down the date your assignment is due, and, if you like, literally draw a picture. For example, to hand in a paper Friday, draw a picture of the paper with "Friday" written on it. You could even draw your future self on Friday, cheering that you've gotten it completed, and thanking yourself for not leaving things to the last minute.

List in detail everything to be done. What steps will get the task completed? For example: research the topic, take notes, make outline, write rough draft, edit rough draft, type final paper, edit final paper. The more detailed your list, the better. If you're uncertain, ask a parent, teacher, or tutor for help.

Schedule each step in reverse. Paper due Friday? Needs editing Thursday, writing Tuesday and Wednesday. Outlining Monday. That means getting all the reading done the weekend before.

be patient with a plan.

Gather everything you need. Finally, make a list of books and supplies required for the task. Books, notes, pens, glue, computer, or whatever else—write that down too.

Remember—never hold a plan in your head. That's burdening your mind unfairly; it takes work keeping track of everything by memory and it's easy to lose track. Write it down and keep it somewhere prominent. Here's an example for a short paper (for a longer paper, you'll need a lot more time):

Friday: Paper is due, hand it in

Thursday: Final edits

Wednesday: Finish writing

Tuesday: Start writing (note to self—at least half of the paper)

Monday: Create an outline

Previous Saturday/Sunday: Research the topic

Prior week: Get books for research

Being kind to yourself means doing things that make your life easier. Because life gets busy and other things come up, create reminders, using sticky notes or phone alarms. Ask someone reliable to help. Alarms and reminders are another way you can be self-compassionate, because they help you get to where you need to go with less mental effort.

Creating a Daily Schedule

Another way to handle time management is creating a daily schedule for yourself. Start by making a list of all the things you need to do. It's often useful to lay out your entire weekly schedule ahead of time.

List everything you need to do, as well as things you want to do, like hobbies. For example:

- School day (including transportation back and forth)

- Homework

- Extracurricular activities and hobbies (sports, music, art, drama)

- Chores

- Sleep (most teens require from nine to ten hours of sleep per night)

- Meditation (at least five minutes)

- Relaxation—"do nothing" time

Schedule everything at a specific time. You can either use an app on your phone or download a planning worksheet at https://www.newharbinger.com/46394. And we mean include *everything*. Put in every chore, assignment, and extracurricular activity—and your fun time and free time too. (As a side note, if there aren't enough hours in the day, it's possible you have too much planned; talk to someone you trust about adjusting your schedule.)

Tip #1: Double your estimate for anything important at first, since ADHD may make you underestimate how long it takes. Seriously. Think math homework takes one hour? Give yourself two until you know for sure. If you think you need fifteen minutes to get ready for school, give yourself thirty. What's the worst that can happen? You end up with extra time on your hands!

Tip #2: Set aside a minimum of fifteen minutes for any task. With ADHD, you may often think, *That will only take a few minutes.* Like, *I only have to throw the brownies for the party together, that'll take five or ten minutes.* Except…you have to find ingredients, bowls, and measuring cups; grease the pan; and…we promise, it adds up to at least fifteen minutes, maybe more. Oh, they probably need to cool for thirty minutes before cutting too.

Tip #3: Schedule transition time between activities. It's easy to forget that moving from one task to another takes time. To arrive at 8:00 for your game, you may need to park at 7:45 to get to the field—and before that, getting ready and driving might take a half hour.

Tip #4: Schedule organizational time. Once a day or once a week, take a few minutes to stay organized. Get rid of papers, put things away, and of course, update your calendar and to-do list.

Break down school assignments into manageable pieces, as you read about in the previous section.

Tip #5: Put each part of a longer assignment into your calendar in daily parts for the week.

Set reminders on your phone ahead of important transitions. You can also put sticky notes in places where you'll see them (the refrigerator door, the computer, or the TV, for example).

Tip #6: Notice any thoughts about why it's okay to skip those alarms. When you catch a thought like that, come back to your feet on the floor for a moment. Picture your future self again, and how you will feel if you leave everything for later.

Reward yourself! When you complete a task, schedule a short break and do something enjoyable. Maybe get up and get moving—put on music and dance, go out for a walk, or kick a soccer ball around.

Tip #7: If you have more work to do, make sure you stick to your plans by setting an alarm to come back after your time is up.

Stay patient with your plan, and problem solve often. Remember, many people with ADHD eventually come to find that, rather than staying focused, their core challenge is managing their time. You will get better at it, but you may try many types of schedules, reminders, and plans before finding what works best.

The same planning might apply to any routine you have. You might, for example, struggle to get out the door on time for the bus. You know what needs to happen but lose track of time and forget your mental to-do list under pressure. So, without judging yourself for that difficulty, make yourself a morning checklist. It works, and it makes life easier.

Figuring out your own best schedule will take time. There are different methods, different styles of day planners, and many good organizational apps. When you fall behind or lose track, start again without beating yourself up. As you now know, self-criticism doesn't help. Remind yourself that you're human, and it's okay if you haven't mastered the right system for you yet.

Social Media: The Ultimate Time Suck

Our phones and computers are useful when it comes to scheduling and reminders, but they can also be distracting. When you're trying to get something done, whether it's schoolwork or chores, interruptions on your phone don't distract you only in that moment. When you come back, it takes about twenty minutes to get your attention fully refocused.

Shifting your attention back and forth from your phone to your work leads to true inefficiency. Some people check their phone hundreds of times daily. It turns out multitasking like that—doing more than one thing at once—is literally impossible; your attention goes into pinball mode. Each shift causes a little lost time, building to a big waste pile of lost time over the course of the day.

Focusing on one thing at a time is more efficient and less prone to errors. It frees up time to later enjoy what you want more fully. Make sure you use your phone—and aren't used by it.

What are some solutions to healthier technology use?

Shut down all unnecessary notifications. Check in on social media when you have time, and *after* you've accomplished whatever has to happen.

Remove all programs you don't need from your phone and devices. Fewer programs means your device runs better (less memory drain) and gives you more privacy (fewer apps tracking everything you do). When it's time to check social media, log in through your browser instead.

Batch your screen time. Whatever you choose to do, set a time limit and elect to do that one activity alone for that period of time. "Monotasking" like this is more effective when you're working and more engaging for fun activities. So you look at your schedule and decide: *I* *have a half hour to check in with my friends online now.* When your timer goes off, pause a bit, then choose what comes next. Most importantly, make a commitment to stay away from your phone when it isn't planned screen time.

Set healthy limits for yourself. Create a phone-free bedtime for yourself, and put your device in another room. It's too tempting to get on your phone and browse all night. Be kind to yourself and get a good night's sleep.

Stay mindful. Practice Three Mindful Breaths before touching your phone. Begin to notice that compulsion to check more, to avoid boredom, or to need another "fix," and start to let go of it. Stay in charge of your actions, rather than your phone. There is research on phone usage suggesting that changes in our brains are similar to the changes found in addicts. Most of us aren't actually addicted…but we all know phones can be pretty disruptive.

Summing It Up

Being kind to yourself means, among other things, doing things that make life easier. Not managing your time well leads to anxiety. Learning to manage your time decreases your stress and helps you feel a whole lot better about yourself.

This chapter included many suggestions for managing time. You deserve to do well and to feel good about yourself. Committing to these suggestions, like using schedules and reminders more consistently, moves you toward your long-term goal of having a successful and less stressful future.

Making your *immediate* future at school less stressful is what the next chapter is about. School can seem way too challenging, so let's dive in and find some tools to make it more manageable and show the world what you're truly capable of.

CHAPTER 8

Succeeding at School
with Less Stress

I'm going to share one of the best pieces of advice I ever got. My junior year English teacher endlessly heard me complain about school and how useless I felt it was. Without even knowing about my ADHD, she said, "You are the kind of person who hates to be bored. You don't have to buy into high school, but you need to get through it. Make sure you go to college so at least you'll have options for a job. How much would you hate being stuck in a job you don't want because you let doors get slammed on you?"

—Jessie, age 21

This chapter is about *you* shifting into gear and getting your car on the road. You want to run your life, and make your own choices? Show the world what you're capable of, and set up your future by getting a handle on school.

Consider this: We tell ourselves stories about ourselves all the time. *I'll be happy once I'm on my own. I'm terrible at sports and I always will be. I suck at math. I'll never remember to use a calendar. I'm not the sort of person who makes lists.*

We define ourselves through such stories, figuring out what we value and who we think we are. These stories aren't by nature right or wrong, or even true or false, but they take on a life of their own. We start to believe them. As a result, they box us in, limiting our possibilities.

Often, however, there is a *kernel* of truth to these stories. Like telling yourself that you don't like to read (which could be true) when what you really dislike are long nonfiction books (which may be more specifically true). So how do your stories, especially ones affected by ADHD, limit you?

For example, is *I'm not the sort of person who makes lists* true of you? What *is* true is that remembering a to-do list may be harder for you than for most people. It may take more of your energy and discipline, and you feel lame because of that. It doesn't mean lists won't *ever* be useful. Living with ADHD may lead you to believe an overly general story about yourself.

Rewrite these stories, though, and guess what? Life gets easier. *I'm not YET the kind of person who uses a to-do list. I find them annoying. I do realize that if it were easier to keep track of things, I'd feel less stressed.* Your ADHD management system needs a bit of a reminder—that's the real story.

The bottom line is this: when we drop the stories we tell ourselves, we open ourselves up to new possibilities.

In this chapter, we'll lay out some practical steps toward quieting your inner critic while managing your academic life with more ease.

The Fakest Storyteller of All: Our Inner Critic

When you have ADHD, you inevitably get corrected a lot by adults. Over time, this can make you feel bad about yourself, like you can't do anything right. You might hear the voice inside your head screaming, "There's no way you can finish this assignment in time. Don't even bother starting." Or "Read the book by the end of the week? Who are you kidding? No way!" When you believe that voice, it undermines your confidence around school.

But if you pause and consider it, your inner critic rarely tells the truth. Those things your inner critic says are only a habitual way of thinking. As you no doubt know by this point, when we view our own mental habits mindfully, we recognize what's true. Our inner critic is part of us, but not one we need to engage with quite so much.

In the moments your critic yells loudest, remember the self-compassion skills you learned in chapter 3. Gently let your critic know it's not being helpful. You might even give it a name, if that helps. "Thanks for your input, Snickerdoodle, but I'm doing everything I can right now." Over time, you will be able to observe that voice of self-criticism without believing it quite so much.

One key to succeeding at school is changing any self-limiting stories you tell yourself about what or who you are. You are not "bad" at school-work, or "bad" at math or English or whatever subjects feel hard for you. You're a person, like any other, who's good at some things and not so good at others.

Many things your mind tells you that you are turn out to be not so permanent after all. It often creates pictures of things you "should" do that aren't really helpful. For example, it may take less effort to keep track of your life in your head, so you think it must be best. Of course, it certainly isn't all that effective a way to keep track of schoolwork.

Learn to be aware of your mind's self-limiting, self-protective patterns. Then create a system for working with what you actually are—a person who happens to have ADHD—in order to achieve what you know you can: success at school.

To get your inner critic to chill, let's learn how you can call a lifeline. In this case, you'll find a compassionate and loving friend surprisingly close by.

FORMAL PRACTICE: **Compassionate Friend**[20]

For this practice, you'll need some imagination—it's a bit like going on a fantasy voyage. You'll find an audio recording at https://www.newharbinger.com/46394. Are you ready?

Either seated or lying down, close your eyes and take a few deep breaths. Allow yourself to relax and let the chair or ground support you. With each breath, see if you can let go and relax a little more.

Now, imagine a place you feel safe, comfortable, and relaxed. It can be a real place or an imagined place, but somewhere that allows you to breathe comfortably and let go of worry. Perhaps it is real, in nature, like a beach, a place in the woods near a brook, a corner of your bedroom, or the comfort of a good friend's house. It might even be an imaginary place, like floating on a cloud.

Imagine this place in as much detail as you can. Enjoy the sounds, smells, physical sensations, and, most of all, what you feel like in this place.

Soon you'll receive a visitor…a warm and kind friend. This is someone who loves you completely and accepts you exactly for who you are.

Maybe this visitor is a real person, like a friend, a grandparent, or a favorite teacher. Or someone from a book you've read, a pet, a superhero, or even a character from a comic book or movie. Or you can create someone in your mind. Imagine this being in detail, especially how it feels to be with them.

Soon you will greet your friend. You have a choice—you can either go out from your safe place to meet them or invite them in. Either is fine; do whichever feels most comfortable. Imagine doing that now.

Now imagine yourself sitting with the person at exactly the right distance away, whatever feels right for you. You feel completely comfortable and safe, completely accepted and loved. This is where you need to be right now.

Take a moment to enjoy how you feel with your special friend. This being is here with you now and understands exactly what it's like to be you, exactly where you are in your life right now, and your struggles.

They know you better than anyone else. They love you unconditionally and accept you completely for who you are. Even when you fail—especially when you fail.

This friend has something important to say to you, something that's *exactly what you need to hear* right now. Listen closely for the words they share, words that are reassuring, supportive, and kind. Maybe something like, "Don't be so hard on yourself. You want to be accepted and loved. That is totally human. We all want that."

If no words come, that's okay too. Just enjoy being with your compassionate friend.

Now, maybe you have something *you'd* like to say to your friend. They are a very good listener, and completely understand you. Is there anything *you'd* like to say?

Enjoy your friend's good company for a few last moments, and wave good-bye to them, knowing you can invite them back whenever you need to.

You are now alone in your safe place again. Spend a few moments reflecting on what happened, and maybe on the words you heard.

Before this practice ends, remember that this compassionate friend is a *part of you*. The loving presence you felt and the words you heard are a deep part of yourself. The comfort and safety that you may have felt is always there within you. Know you can return to this safe place and compassionate friend whenever you need to.

Now bring your attention back to your breath. When you feel ready, gently open your eyes.

You may have been surprised that you have this lifeline within you. We all have this voice, our compassionate friend, inside us. It may be hidden or quiet, but it is there nonetheless, a voice that is kind, loving, and supportive whenever we need it.

Our task, then, is to nurture that kind voice until it becomes strong, resilient, and easier to hear. We do this by continuing our self-compassion practice.

A New Storyline Around School:
Less Stress, More Success

We'll soon focus on what you can do to take control of your schoolwork. Before we start…

Question your stories. Whenever a self-limiting thought comes up, dig inside yourself and ask: *Is it really true? How do I know?* Suppose you didn't get chosen for the debate team, and it was something that felt really important. You might tell yourself it's because the teacher in charge doesn't like you. Ask yourself: *Do I know this is true without a doubt? Could there be some other explanation?*

Another useful idea to know about (though you can forget the actual term if you want) is *growth mind-set*. Growth mind-set means believing that your intelligence and learning develop through your own effort, and by trying different learning strategies and asking for help when you need it. Research has shown that if you have a growth mind-set, you're more likely to do better in school.[21] Put in the work (like some of the ways shown in this book), and you can become more successful.

On the other hand, a *fixed mind-set* boxes you in with self-limiting stories. *I'm not smart enough. Only As are good enough. I'll never make the team, so why bother trying?* Of course, it's great to have a realistic view of our abilities. But when we decide our success relies on something out of our control, we'll quit more quickly when the going gets tough. When we give up and believe these stories, that fixed mind-set gets in the way of our success.

Keep track of nothing in your head. With ADHD, it's super hard to remember things. You may try holding your homework assignments and test reminders in your head sometimes. *It's fine, I'll remember that for sure.* It's annoying to consider something as boring as keeping a to-do list, but that's because it's hard to keep track of that list in the first place. Your ADHD brain manager says, "Leave me alone, lists are annoying." But the part that knows you can do better probably has a sneaking suspicion that to-do lists can help.

When you juggle things in your head, details get lost. It's tiring and true for anyone, but worse with ADHD. So make it easy on yourself. Write down everything that needs to happen. Use a list on your phone, if that's simpler. Most come with a to-do list built in, and various free programs add all sorts of bells and whistles. You know why there are so many to-do list apps? Because *everyone* has trouble keeping track of stuff!

Here's a key rule to staying on top of schoolwork: either do what needs to get done *immediately* or write it down somewhere *immediately*. That's all.

The Shortest Path to Effective Studying

In college, I started dating this guy, and he was great at school. I mean, he mastered the art of studying. I didn't even know there was a way I was supposed to be doing it! Once he showed me, school got so much easier. My grades went up, and the work actually felt less hard than it did before.

—Anna, age 19

As with many things, how to study is easy to describe, but *making* yourself study is hard. While true for all students, getting a handle on *how* to study makes things easier when you have ADHD. The trick is this: For each class, create a *specific* plan before you start. For any class or new project, make sure you have an idea for how to best learn the material or complete the work. Then *reinforce* that approach until it becomes routine. Stay patient when implementing your plan, because study habits become effortless only over time.

It's pretty common not to want to study, or to forget. But having strong study habits is like maintaining your car. It may not be as dazzling as a brand-new one, but if you stay on top of the oil changes and tune-ups, your car will run better. When you stay on top of your school-work, you'll do better in school with less effort...so it is another way of being kind to yourself. Maybe not as exciting as your favorite hobby or hanging out with your friends, but it is strong life maintenance.

Maintaining strong study habits starts with four general concepts:

Study a small amount each day, instead of a large amount all at once. Information sticks better when broken up over time, with less last-minute stress. Fifteen minutes a day over four days is the same amount of time as one hour at the last minute. But fifteen minutes a day helps you remember more in the long run. For a challenging class, try to find a few minutes nightly to review; even five or ten minutes helps.

Focus on what's hard first. Our brains often trick us. Often, we review what we know (prob-ably because it is reassuring to us) and we don't study what's hard (probably because... well...it's hard). We feel less short-term stress as we are avoiding the boring work. But of course, that means studying for the harder stuff when we're tired late at night, or we run out of time and end up not doing it at all. When you catch yourself, tackle difficult tasks early *even though you don't want to.* If you're using flashcards, for example, create one pile of what you know, and one that feels harder. Come back from time to time to the easy cards and repeat the harder stack until you have it down cold. It's the only way to make sure you do as well as you're able.

Get enough sleep. We know, we know, sleep probably sounds as boring as studying. But it's another case of a short-term choice that makes things easier in the long term. Sleeping enough on a school night makes it far more likely you'll do well with your tests and assignments the next day. You'll also remember and retain what you've learned. Your *hippocampus*—the part of your brain responsible for learning and memory—needs sleep to move what you've learned into your long-term memory. Without enough sleep (and believe it or not, the average amount of sleep that teens need is nine and one-quarter hours), what you've learned goes by the wayside.

Ask for help. The sooner you find help with a challenging topic, the sooner you move past it. Growth mind-set includes trying multiple strategies to learn and asking for help when you need it. Trying your best means being aware of when something is confusing and responding by asking someone to help sort it out with you.

So that's a general approach to studying. What many people (even adults) don't know is that there are specific proven strategies too. Because subjects at school require different kinds of learning—like memorizing, analyzing, summarizing, writing, problem solving—different strategies exist for different kinds of learning. For example, to learn the different parts of your skeletal system would likely require memorization. To write a synopsis of a novel for English would require higher level skills like summarizing. You'll make your own life easier if you know where to turn when a subject gets challenging:

Classes that require memorization—use flashcards. Online quizzes and games are good too, but writing the cards out by hand helps you learn. Keep two stacks, one you have down cold, and one to keep working on. Don't believe us? Handwrite a hard spelling word five times and see what happens.

Classes that require problem solving, like math or science—use practice problems. The best practice includes explanations of what you have gotten wrong.

Classes that require in-depth thought and comprehension—take notes. Some classes, like history or science, require analyzing topics or books. Whether reading a chapter or sitting in class, try taking notes. Notes taken by hand rather than on a computer are usually remembered better. (Then again, it is common for handwriting to be overwhelming and unreadable when you have ADHD, so type notes if you need to.) Later, after you've read the chapter outside of class time, consider creating concise outlines from your notes. Because note taking relies on your brain manager, you may want to connect with someone who can teach you a note-taking method, such as the Cornell Note Taking System.

Writing Made Simple(r)

Writing was so intense! Everyone said I was the best writer in the class, but it took me forever. I'd write, like, ten pages and then spend days cutting it down to the two my teacher wanted.

—Natalie, age 16

Writing is often very, very hard for many people with ADHD, and, unfortunately, the way to make it easier often seems like an annoying waste of time. Your ADHD brain manager says, *Ugh, making an outline is dumb. I want to go have fun.* But that's only because your brain manager doesn't find planning your writing natural yet. It feels useful only once it becomes an effortless routine.

Now let's listen to that other voice, the one deep inside that wants you to do well. It may even have an inkling of what might work better. That voice says something like, *Well, I guess if organizing saves me stress I could try it, even though it is a bore.* It feels like an extra, time-wasting step, but getting your thoughts together first makes both the writing and the editing faster.

An outline is like a GPS. It lays out a step-by-step plan of what you will say and when. When you include lots of detail in your outline, your writing becomes nothing more than tying it together. Novelists and screenwriters outline even the most convoluted and complex plots first. Even comic book writers create detailed outlines before they start writing or drawing!

Guess what? We used an outline to write this book. We titled every chapter, and under that we made bullet points about everything we planned to cover. That was before our editors would even look at our ideas! And then they suggested a few changes, so we edited our outline. Only then did we start writing. As we wrote the chapters, we adjusted our outline because as you write, what you want to say may shift a bit.

Outlining, like note taking, is another idea that is simple to describe, and complicated to learn. It takes persistence to figure out what works. Once again, stay patient with yourself until you discover a useful system that works for you, or find someone who can teach you an approach that works for you.

So here's the plan: Outline first. Save time. Write better. Stress less.

One Last Step: Getting to the Finish Line

One common experience with ADHD is that you set out to do exactly what you need to do but don't quite get to the last step. You complete your homework, start thinking about dinner, and forget to put your homework in your backpack. Or you begin to clean up after dinner, get a text from a friend, and never return to cleaning up. Something comes up, you get distracted, and before you know it, you're doing something else altogether and you never get to the finish line.

INFORMAL PRACTICE: **STOP**

STOP is another in-the-moment mindfulness practice to avoid falling into that pitfall, so you can actually follow through to the end. Right when you're going from one activity to the next, remember the acronym STOP:

- **S**top what you are doing.
- **T**ake three slow mindful breaths.
- **O**bserve what is going on around you, and in your mind.
- **P**ick the right thing to do next.

As a start, set a reminder for yourself. For example, a STOP sticker on your homework folder will signal you to do the STOP practice before leaving your desk.

This STOP practice gets used in many ways. You can do it during any transition during your day, like getting dressed or starting schoolwork or a chore. When you finish your homework, you see the STOP sticker you put on your folder. Pause and check in. *Have I really completed my homework? Have I put it in my backpack? Is my backpack by the door ready for me to grab as I go out the door in the morning?* If the answer is yes to all those questions, then ta-da! Done!

A STOP helps with a messy room. Put a STOP sticker on your bedroom door. You're getting dressed, ready to go out, and...STOP. The last step to getting dressed is putting your other clothes away or in the hamper. It's not hard to handle only one or two items on the floor. One pair of socks tossed into the laundry is nothing, but picking up ankle-deep clothing a few weeks later feels overwhelming.

These STOP reminders, whether stickers or something else, can live anywhere you know you have trouble remembering. Like all of us, you will sometimes forget. These mindfulness practices can help build your ability to pause, notice what's going on, and act in ways that will make your life easier in the long run.

Asking for Help When You Need It

Consider what advice you would give a friend who wants to go to college on a tennis scholarship. They have to keep getting better at tennis to qualify. First, they need to practice a lot. And then they need to commit to learning new skills from their coach, rather than hitting the ball any way *they* want. That's obvious and sound advice.

Now come back to your goals. You want to be successful and independent. And yet, your ADHD has gotten in the way of the skills you need—so far. Like your tennis-playing friend, you need to put effort into practicing habits that will help you succeed in school, at your extracurriculars, with your friends, and in life. You want strong coaches, like your parents and your teachers, who want to help you up your game so eventually you achieve your goals.

One way to build the skills that let you thrive is finding someone you trust to work with. There's no point struggling alone. Asking for help is a skill of its own. Confident adults ask for help on the job, seeking out someone more experienced for assistance in a project, for example. Without asking questions, they might mess up. At home, adults lean on friends for advice and emotional support, and arrange help with child care or even household chores when they can afford it.

Being kind to yourself means reaching out to others—perhaps a parent, a counselor, or even a specialist in ADHD—around the things that you struggle with. Truth be told, working with a specialist is one of the most proven ways to overcome your ADHD. Think about it this way: You want to be independent of adults, and to be successful. Connecting with an ADHD expert who can show you the way may get you to that goal fastest.

Okay, that was a lot to consider. And if you're like a lot of teens (especially those with ADHD), you sometimes want to move. Run, dance, take a walk, and burn off some energy. And guess what? That can be a mindfulness practice too.

So often we do something that could be relaxing while lost in our thoughts. Maybe we go for a run and dwell over an argument the whole time. We miss out on the run entirely.

When we're being mindful, we put relaxed effort into paying attention to whatever we're doing. That might mean the feeling of a breeze, our feet on the ground, smells, and, quite importantly (if we don't want to bump into something), the sights. What follows is one way to practice mindfulness while stretching. At https://www.newharbinger.com/46394, you'll find an audio recording of this practice.

INFORMAL PRACTICE: **Mindful Movement**

Stand with your feet about a foot apart from each other, and your arms at your sides. Next, stretch your arms and hands straight up, reaching toward the sky, keeping both feet firmly planted on the floor. Reach with your arms and hands as high as you can. Notice how your body feels as you do this. Notice which muscles feel stretched.

Now, making fists with your hands, circle your wrists so that your hands make circles in one direction. Do this for about a minute. Notice the sensations in your wrists and hands as you do this. Now circle them in the opposite direction for about a minute.

Shake out your arms and wrists and hands, and put them at your sides.

Next, with your left hand on your hip, stretch your right arm up and over your head, stretching the right side of your body. As you do, notice how the right side of your body feels. Notice every little sensation that comes up.

Standing upright again, notice how your two sides feel; one has been stretched—the right side—and one hasn't: the left side. Notice how they feel the same and how they feel different. Take some time to absorb how these physical sensations differ.

Now stretch your left side, in the same way that you stretched your right side. Stretch your left arm over your head, arching it and bending it to the right. Notice how stretching your left side feels.

Now come back to standing, with both arms at your sides. Let your shoulders and arms relax, and notice if you want to wriggle your hands for a few seconds before letting them relax.

Take a few slow, relaxing breaths, allowing each out-breath to let you sink a little more into your body. When you're ready, end your practice and decide what you want to do next with your day.

You can practice mindfulness like this during any physical activity. Walking from one place to another, you can stay caught up in busy thoughts or focus on what you see, hear, and feel while walking. Give your mind a break and give yourself some space from your thoughts. Gather your awareness, and give your attention to jogging or swimming or yoga.

Any time you actively decide to apply focus and awareness can be a mindfulness practice. And when you practice mindfulness, it makes every part of dealing with your ADHD easier, through noticing what might be distracting you, seeing what you need to do, and waking up your sleepy brain manager.

Summing It Up

So where in your ADHD journey are you? Hopefully you're starting to recognize, and practice, self-compassion. And to accept and manage your ADHD both in general, in your day-to-day life, and in specific contexts, like at school. Both are possible.

When you have ADHD, it is easy to see yourself as a certain kind of student. That story doesn't have to be true. You can reframe it. You may be having a hard time with focus or planning, but that can change. One first step is recognizing that you are valued and valuable, and just fine the way you are.

Like everyone else, you have a challenge to handle. Drop your story line. See what needs to be done, and then make it happen.

CHAPTER 9

Taking Care of Your Health

Honestly, I felt run—down all the time and didn't know it could be different. Everything felt like it took too much energy to bother. If I had free time, I wanted to lie on the couch and binge—watch shows. It kind of became a way of life. It's amazing how much happier and more energetic I am now that I'm watching out for my health.

—Tama, age 18

There's an old story that goes something like this: A great leader travels through the jungle to find a teacher who knows the meaning of life and how to be a skilled leader. After days of hard travel, she gets to the cave and the teacher won't speak at all.

The leader pleads, "I've been traveling for days. Please don't turn me away."

Finally, the teacher gives in. She says, "The meaning of it all is this: treat everyone how you would like to be treated."

The leader frowns. "I've traveled all this way for that? Even a four-year-old knows that."

To which the teacher responds, "Of course! It's easy at four. It's hard at fourteen, or forty."

In the same way, you don't need another lecture or list about how to be healthy. There's no great new wisdom to share. Living a healthy life often doesn't involve knowing more than you already know.

What matters instead is exploring why we don't always do what we know is best. We get into ruts that feel impossible to break. We mindlessly drift into autopilot and don't consider our daily choices. And when we're down on ourselves, we don't always believe we deserve better.

The solution? As you may have guessed by now, mindfulness and self-compassion. Related to health, that means observing with curiosity, and without self-judgment, how healthy your habits are...and actively seeking to make the changes you need.

Here's a motivational wake-up call to start: Undermanaged ADHD has been connected to a shorter life span. Having ADHD creates *other* health risks, ranging from a sedentary lifestyle to substance abuse to obesity. ADHD symptoms like inattention, difficulty sustaining effort, impulsiveness, emotional reactivity, and problems with time management get in the way of your health routines.

ADHD's impact on health also can make your ADHD symptoms worse. That creates a vicious cycle. ADHD undermines habits like exercise, eating well, and sleep. When these health routines get disrupted, it gets harder to focus, manage emotions, and handle life in general. Establishing a healthier lifestyle, incorporating elements of what we suggest next, lessens the impact of your ADHD.

Additionally, your emotional well-being relies on your physical lifestyle. Activities like exercise seem optional, but our bodies don't think so. No one feels good or thinks clearly when physically run-down. Of course, how we treat ourselves is easily overlooked when we're in a low energy rut. We're burned out and want to do even less. But it's often getting exercise or quality sleep that breaks us out of our funk. Staying resilient relies on strong health habits.

You deserve a healthy future and can make it happen. Treating yourself well means identifying what's best for you instead of staying stuck in old routines. In this chapter, we'll explore how new habits of eating, sleeping, exercise, and outdoor time make you feel better and are another opportunity for you to be kind to yourself. We'll also explore common misunderstandings about ADHD medication, so that you can better decide if you might find it useful. Living better comes down to establishing new habits. Keep moving toward them, patiently, a step at a time.

Here are some things to consider.

Nutrition

Over time, we all develop habits around how we eat. We consume foods we like so quickly we hardly taste them. We buy certain foods or drinks because that's what we always do at the store. Some of us eat when anxious or angry, believing it helps us calm down. But the brief joy of eating junk results in only temporary happiness, and then we're back dealing with the same anxiety and anger.

With ADHD, poor eating habits, obesity, and eating disorders become more common. It's way more complicated than getting distracted when eating. When your brain manager isn't fully on the job, it leads to habits like overeating, emotional eating, or impulse shopping.

See your ADHD clearly and do something about it. Once you're aware that you're eating too fast, or that what you're eating isn't the healthiest for you, you can overcome that pattern. Next, let's explore a mindful eating practice, because greater awareness will let you enjoy your food more and eat more healthily too.

FORMAL PRACTICE: **Mindful Eating**

You can do this with a small piece of fruit, like a raisin, strawberry, or grape, or a piece of mandarin orange. At https://www.newharbinger.com/46394, you'll find an audio recording of this practice. If you are reading the practice instead of listening, take your time with each of your senses as they are introduced.

Pretend you've arrived from another planet on this little place called Earth. You open your hand, and lo and behold, this object lands on it. You have no idea what it is, having never seen it before.

First explore it with your sense of sight. What do you see? Give attention to the details, like colors, shadows, and light.

What does your sense of touch tell you about this object? Is it light, heavy, or dense? Smooth or rough? Warm or cold?

Now using your nose, how would you describe this object? Does it have a smell?

Are you noticing any changes in your mouth as you explore this object? Do you notice your mouth salivating? Or is it dry?

Next, use your sense of hearing. Roll this object next to your ear. What do you hear? Try both ears. Is it different from one ear to the other?

Remember, you can't compare this object to anything on earth because you're unfamiliar with everything here. Simply observe, noting each of your senses as you explore.

Now place it in your mouth and let it sit there for a moment. Notice what you're feeling and thinking. What's the texture in your mouth? Notice sensations as you hold it briefly in your mouth.

Notice the taste before you take a bite. How would you describe it?

Now take a bite. What happens?

Slowly, turn the bite over in your mouth, noticing texture and taste. It's best to do this silently, and it's sometimes easier with your eyes closed.

Choose when to swallow. Finally, what role is your tongue playing right now?

As you finish this practice, ask yourself: *What is it like to pay this much attention to something I'm eating? How was this experience different from the way I normally eat?* And consider for a moment: What would it be like if you paid this much attention to other aspects of life? Schoolwork or sports? Listening to music? Conversations? What would it be like to pay this much attention to yourself and your feelings in times of stress?

Shifting toward healthy eating habits is easiest when you take one small step at a time. You might pick one food you eat a lot of that isn't all that good for you, like Doritos, and swap it out for pretzels. Or maybe decide to eat fruit after dinner if that time is when you crave sweets. Reach your long-term goals by taking one small, realistic step at a time, and then taking one more.

How you eat matters too. Eating slowly allows your body to pick up cues that it is full. The signal between your belly and your brain takes a while. Anything that slows you down helps. You can practice putting your utensil down between bites, or taking smaller portions before deciding if you need more. And of course, you taste your food more when you slow down.

To stay in the driver's seat means making active, self-compassionate choices instead of falling into ruts. It's more difficult than it seems, in part because an entire industry spends hundreds of millions of dollars getting teens to buy their products. They want you to eat their food and drink their sodas, and to believe their stuff makes you happier. Taking control of life means seeing through the marketing and actively choosing the way you want to live.

For all the best-selling books and opinionated online voices, there's no mystery about what's best for your body. Radical diets are rarely good for you and most often impossible to sustain. Unless you have an underlying health condition requiring a specific diet, the best way to eat is a well-balanced variety of food. Lots of fruits and veggies, some protein, and a minimum of junk food and sweets.

But you know all that diet advice, right? You've heard it your whole life! Ultimately, the key is compassion for yourself. Respect yourself enough to put the effort into improving how you eat, without judging yourself for how you eat now. Like all of us, you can then make slow, steady changes over time that help you feel healthy and strong.

Sleep

All I can say is, it took me years—I was halfway through college—before I stopped staying up all night. And it was like a whole new world for me. I didn't feel foggy all day anymore. And I was happier too, for sure.

—Anita, age 20

ADHD makes it hard to fall asleep, and sometimes also difficult to stay asleep; your mind gets going and you're up later than you want. It can be hard to settle your mind and body at night when ADHD causes busy thinking, fidgeting, and impulsiveness. Your mind runs through everything that happened that day or worries what might happen the next—especially when external distractions go away and you're alone lying in bed. All of that makes it hard to relax and fall asleep. Plus, getting to bed both on time and in a peaceful environment helps with sleep, and ADHD makes those details more challenging too—that's because keeping track of time and keeping your room organized are both harder with ADHD.

ADHD also puts you at a slight risk for something called a sleep disorder. That's a medical condition interfering with sleep, like snoring related to sleep apnea, or restless leg syndrome. If you never feel rested no matter how much sleep you get, talk to your doctor. See if it's possible something else is going on that needs treatment.

As a first step toward better sleep, figure out how much you need. By this, we mean the amount you get naturally, *after* a few days of catching up on any sleep you might've missed. It's typically the number of hours you sleep when you're on a vacation. For most teens, as you read earlier, that means somewhere between nine and ten hours a day. It's easy to pretend that you can get by with less, but to be at your best, you want to operate on a full tank. Sleep lets your brain run smoothly.

Right now, try a brief mindfulness practice, exploring what tiredness feels like. Bring attention to the physical sensations in your body. Notice the feeling in your head, particularly around your eyes. Maybe if you're tired you feel a little buzzing or vibrating somewhere in your body. What's your mental state? Is it sharp and alert, or sluggish and irritated?

Some other time when you're fully rested, maybe after a long weekend, try the same practice again. Overall, how does your body feel when rested? Your head and eyes? What are your thoughts like when you're rested, and your emotions? Do you see any differences?

If you want to sleep more easily, hard as it may be, find a routine that works for you. If you carve out a new routine for settling down at night, your body adapts to that consistent plan. Because your body clock and your schedule start to match, you'll fall asleep more easily. You'll sleep better and feel more rested.

Here are some ways to establish an easier sleep routine:

Create a peaceful sleep environment. Set up a quiet, dark, and uncluttered setting. For some people, sound machines are helpful—they block out outside noise and are soothing.

Make your bedtime the same every night. Your body gets accustomed to falling asleep at a certain time when your bedtime is consistent. Most people experience a stretch of time nightly during which it is easiest to fall asleep. Get into bed too early, and you're restless and awake. But stay up too late, and you pass through the window where your body is ready for sleep and are up for another couple of hours. Aim to turn out the lights at the time when your body is most prepared to shut down for the night.

Engage in a short restful activity or two before bed. Choose activities that slow down your mind and body. Reading a few pages (not on a screen) before you go to bed or listening to gentle music can help. Or do a body scan. (You'll read about this in a bit.)

Put your screens out of your bedroom. Screens of any kind—computers, TVs, and phones—disrupt sleep both because they are mentally engaging and because they emit a type of light that interferes with sleep. This light delays the release of melatonin, a natural chemical that makes you sleepy before bedtime. To feel rested, skip screens for at least one to two hours before you want to sleep.

Avoid drinking anything that disrupts sleep near bedtime. The most common one in older teens is caffeine, which is found in soda, coffee, and even chocolate. Some people can't sleep well if they have any caffeine at all after lunchtime.

Practice mindfulness. Far too often, when we're having a hard time falling asleep, our mind gets even busier. We're waiting to fall asleep and start to review all the things that we're worrying about. In other words, we dive into thinking about the past or future. That keeps us awake. Mindfulness practice brings us back and allows us to let go of those worries, which makes sleep easier.

In fact, a particular meditation practice called the body scan settles the energy in the body and makes it easier to fall asleep. The Mindfulness in Schools project calls these body scans "beditation"! Let's try it now. At https://www.newharbinger.com/46394, you'll find an audio recording of the practice.

FORMAL PRACTICE: **Body Scan**

To begin, lie down on your back and gently close your eyes, fully or partially. Allow your arms to rest by your sides, about six inches away from your body, and allow your legs to rest in a relaxed manner.

Turn your attention to your breath, and see if you can notice it moving gently in and out of your body. Notice your belly rising and falling with each in-breath and each out-breath.

Now shift your attention from your belly all the way down to your feet. Notice any sensations in your feet. Are they warm or cool, dry or moist? Can you feel the touch of your feet against the bed, or the floor?

As you inhale, shift your attention from your feet up into your ankles, calves, and shins. Let go of any unnecessary effort. Let it be easy.

If you notice your mind has wandered, as it may after a few moments, return to the sensations in your body.

Now, returning to your legs, simply be aware of sensations of pressure, contact, or numbness. If there's any sense of tension or tightness, see if you can let go a little. Relax that part of your body as much as you can.

Now shift your attention to your knees, thighs, and hips, noticing what sensations are here. If you experience discomfort, like restlessness or an itch, see what changes if you observe that discomfort without immediately doing anything. Always take care of yourself, though. If something causes too much discomfort, notice that, pause a moment, and then make whatever adjustment seems most appropriate.

Shifting now into your belly, be aware of your body breathing and feeling your breath expanding and contracting as you breathe. Notice your breath as a sensation in your body. Notice sensations within your belly, like fullness or hunger. Your belly is one place you might feel an emotion too. If you do, what does it feel like? Butterflies? Nausea? Something else?

And now, shift your attention to your chest, noticing it rising and falling with each breath, or your heart beating. Simply feeling your body as it is. Perhaps bringing a sense of gratitude to your lungs and heart for all they do to keep you alive.

Guide your attention now to your hands. Nothing you need to do with them— simply noticing temperature or touch. Letting go again of tightness if they feel tense. And then, after a few moments, moving at a leisurely pace through your lower arms. And then your upper arms. And then your shoulders.

Shift your awareness now to your lower back. Notice any sensations here. Noticing, perhaps, the movement of your back with each breath. When you're ready, moving to your middle back. Feeling that sense of pressure against the surface you're on. What does the point of contact feel like against your back? Now moving to your upper back, a place where many of us hold tension. Relaxing your upper back, allowing it to sink into the floor or bed a little more with each exhale.

Now, shifting your attention to your neck, throat, and head. Notice in particular any sense of tightness or tension in the muscles of your face. Seeing if, perhaps, you can soften those muscles a little.

Now that you have paid attention to each individual part of your body, broaden your awareness to your whole body. As much as feels comfortable, relaxing a little bit more, letting go a little more.

If you'd like, take a moment for yourself, and then choose when to sit up. Or continue with the practice while allowing your body to relax and fall asleep.

Physical Exercise

Exercise has been described as the only magic pill in life. It has increasingly been linked with not only physical but also mental health. We may get the message from our society that exercise is optional. Some people do it, some don't. But really, your body is like an expensive car, needing care and attention. The human body is designed for movement; consistent exercise keeps you at your best.

Interestingly, people with ADHD typically exercise less than people who don't have it, even though exercise helps alleviate ADHD symptoms. We know without a doubt that exercise is linked to emotional resilience, learning, happiness, and improved ADHD symptoms. It also lowers the risk of depression in teens. Being kind and self-compassionate means keeping physical activity part of your life. How you exercise is optional, whether you exercise isn't.

Beware, though. If you haven't been exercising, it won't feel good at first—which makes it more likely you'll stop again. So start with small steps. Even five minutes a day helps. And keep your eyes on the prize: Once your body gets used to exercise again, it releases endorphins when you work out. Once that happens, exercise feels good.

Despite knowing that exercise matters, most people report not having time for it. When researchers track how they spend their hours, however, guess what? It turns out they do *literally* have time for exercise, they only *believe* they don't. Much of that lost time gets spent on—you guessed it—screens.

If you believe something similar, being aware of how you use your time is a moment of mindfulness in itself: you make an assumption (*I have no time*) and notice a habit you have (*I'm not exercising much*). Seen that way, the assumption turns out to be only an inaccurate thought, and the habit isn't as fixed and permanent as it seems. As always, awareness is the first step toward making a change.

One common tip that might help: Develop a routine. Whatever you choose to do, do it the same time each day. Start with fifteen minutes. That regular exercise will eventually feel good. For real.

Try thinking of a fun way to exercise. In fact, don't even call it exercise. Are you the sort of person who likes socializing? Do you prefer indoor or outdoor activities? Choose something enjoyable, and you'll stick with your commitment longer. If you feel like exercise can't ever be fun, explore that perception as well—is it true? Then come back to what you know is best for yourself. Plan to move and see what happens.

Here are some ideas, though this list by no means includes all types of exercise:

Dance—put on music and dance in your room, or take lessons in modern dance, jazz, tap, or hip-hop. Or get creative and make up your own dance style.

Play a sport or practice on your own—basketball, tennis, running, baseball, soccer, skating, volleyball, or swimming.

Go biking or hiking, alone or with a group.

How about yoga, tai chi, or qigong?

Try exercise programs online—you never have to leave home!

Getting Outdoors

Did you know that time outdoors in nature has been linked to better moods, feeling more restored, experiencing less anxiety and depression, and thinking more clearly? Hard to believe, right? So get your butt in gear and take it outside.

No one knows exactly why, but there seems to be a basic biological need that is met when you're out in nature. We're not suggesting that you scale a mountain…even lying on your back on a blanket in your backyard or sitting on a park bench works. Here are some ways you can be mindful in nature without going too far from your home. Remember, when your mind wanders, gently bring your attention back.

Climb a tree. (Remember doing that as a kid?) Notice the feel of the bark as you're climbing, and the sensation of the bark against your back.

Lie in your backyard and look at clouds. Simply enjoy the shapes and movement as they pass.

Go outside at night and stare at the stars.

Go for a hike. (There are websites for local, state, and national parks.) For at least five minutes on the hike, be silent and pay attention to what's around you.

If you live in a city, find a public park. Sit on a bench for a while and people watch. Do nothing else (in other words, no phone!). Or walk through the park, paying attention to the trees, flowers, people, or whatever else is around you.

Sit outside in a place where you can pay attention to the sounds of birds. Simply listen to the birds without doing anything else.

Sit outside somewhere and notice the feeling of the air on your skin.

Whenever I start feeling a little antsy, I've learned it's time to go outside. I take my dog, Rocket, and we walk down to the park near my apartment building. Rocket loves the smells, and I walk around and follow his lead. Being there makes me feel better.

—Maya, age 16

Driving

The #1 cause for death in teens is accidents. Over a third of them happen in motor vehicles. Research has shown that ADHD puts you at higher risk for car accidents, and on top of that, teens take greater risks when with friends in the car than when alone. What does this mean for you? Stay aware when you're behind the wheel, and notice the choices you make when driving, particularly any urge to take risks when your friends are with you in the car. Bottom line is, don't do things that you wouldn't otherwise do.

Paying attention to everything around you when driving is obviously key to your safety and the safety of everyone else on the road around you. This means signs, lights, other cars, and tons more. There's a lot for your brain manager to keep track of while driving!

These steps can help you get ready to drive mindfully:

As you sit in the driver's seat and before you start the car, notice the feeling of your hands on the steering wheel. Notice whether the wheel is cold to your touch, or warm. Is it rough or smooth? Hard or cushiony?

Take three mindful breaths, noticing your breath as it comes in through your nose and into your lungs, and then out again.

Maybe notice the urge to move, to leave your driveway or parking spot and start your trip. Where in your body do you feel that urge? What does it feel like?

See if you can stay with that urge for a full ten seconds—without acting on it yet.

Now as you start your car, listen to the sound of the motor. Before moving, spend a few seconds—at least five—listening to the sound of the motor.

Proceed on your way.

Remember, whenever you're stopped at a light you can bring your attention back to the feeling of your hands on the steering wheel.

Remaining aware of everything around you when driving creates a safe driving experience for you, whoever is in the car with you, other drivers, and pedestrians. Create an environment within the car that keeps you safe and focused. That might mean being stricter with yourself around texting, goofing around, or anything else distracting. Splitting your attention never works, and you don't need us to tell you the potential consequences of not paying attention while driving.

ADHD and Medication

Starting ADHD medication was radical. It was like the curtains going up on life. Before, it was like everyone around me had been riding motor-cycles and I was still riding my bike. When I take my meds, I'm moving at the same pace as everyone else, and it's awesome.

—Joseph, age 17

Okay, let's be honest. Few people want to take medication for any reason. And no one should who doesn't require it. On the other hand, some teens refuse medication even when their health depends on it. For example, some teens who have diabetes, having been dependent on insulin throughout childhood, resist taking that medicine when they're teens. And their life depends on it! So what gives?

There are likely a number of reasons. Probably some of it has to do with the need teens have to be independent. Totally understandable, as it is literally a teen's "job" to become independent from parents.

But as you're becoming more independent, make sure you care for yourself. You deserve it. That means making decisions based on what is most helpful and healthy for you. Becoming a healthy adult requires just that—making tough decisions that put you on the road to functioning at your best.

ADHD is a medical disorder. That doesn't mean you *must* take medication, but that is why medication works for many with ADHD. Without it, many people can't focus or control their impulses. And the reality is that nearly eight out of ten people can benefit from medication, and without significant side effects, meaning without changes in eating, sleeping, emotions, or creativity.

Mindfulness is about seeing life clearly and objectively, and that can be helpful when considering medication. There is often a lot of misinformation about ADHD medication. In spite of what you may have heard, it has been around nearly one hundred years and is safe when used appropriately. When you come across an odd fact around medication, check your source, and ask yourself, *Is this something I know to be true?*

There are a number of myths around ADHD medications. Here are the facts:

- ADHD medications are not a crutch, a cheat, or a performance enhancer, any more than insulin is for diabetes or asthma medication is for that condition. Used appropriately, ADHD medication provides a support for your brain that helps you manage life.

- Using medication does *not* make you more likely to need it as you grow older. In fact, if you use medications when you're young, you may be *less* likely to need them as an adult.[22]

- ADHD medication does not increase your risk of substance abuse and is not addictive if used appropriately. In fact, it's having untreated ADHD that puts you at risk for substance abuse.[23]

- ADHD medications do not affect your creativity or your personality. If you feel they do, it probably means you're on the wrong medication.

Whether to take medication is a big decision you should probably discuss with an adult you trust. Talk with a parent, as well as a doctor or another professional. If you decide to try medication, here are a few guidelines:

Aim for absolutely no side effects. Any time you make a medication change, use your mindfulness practice to check in with how you feel. Mild appetite loss is hard to avoid, but otherwise, you shouldn't have any side effects—physically or emotionally. If you do, ask your doctor to change your medication.

Work with your doctor to get the dose right. You will probably need to try a few different doses until you find the right amount for full benefits. To monitor the dose well, know that medications help primarily with symptoms related to focus, hyperactivity, and impulsiveness. If you're on the right dose, those symptoms bother you much less. Other parts of executive function, like time management or organization, don't typically improve much with medication. Lastly, people with ADHD tend to underestimate their symptoms, so try to get someone you trust, like your parent or teachers, to see if they notice a difference in your behavior, emotions, or motivation.

Work with your doctor to get the timing right. Make sure the medications cover your whole day, including after-school activities and homework. Bigger doses don't necessarily last longer. If you need more of your day covered, you need a new medication that lasts longer or a second dose later in the day.

Use the medications every day. ADHD does not affect only school, as you now know. If you don't take your medication every day, you are more likely to be distracted and watch TV, rather than doing something healthy for yourself such as a new fun project, getting outdoors, or hanging out with friends. Staying on your medication helps you manage your own health, social life, driving, and more.

Unfortunately, the reality of ADHD medication is that you may have to try many of them before you find what makes you feel best. Collaborate with your doctor to make that happen. Any time you feel like you are still struggling with your ADHD, it may be time to talk about adjusting your ADHD medication.

Truthfully, when you're on the right medication at the right dose, ADHD medications are more likely to help than any other single treatment. Not just that, but most importantly, you'll feel like the best version of yourself. Properly used, ADHD medications can be life changing.

Summing It Up

When you practice mindfulness and self-compassion, you learn to value yourself and realize that others should value you too. And that means, among other things, that you deserve to feel relatively happy and headed toward success. Of course, you're not going to be happy all the time, because that's not realistic. You do, however, want to travel down a road where your life feels manageable. One way to steer yourself this way is through wholesome habits around eating, sleep, and exercise; getting outdoors as much as you can; and using ADHD medications well. Stay aware of what your body needs, stay kind to yourself, and you will lead yourself into a full and fulfilling future.

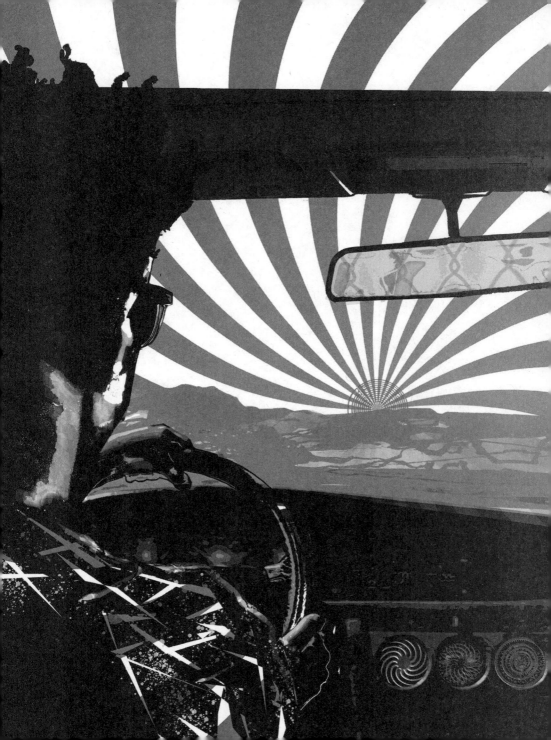

CHAPTER 10

Steering Yourself to the Future You Choose

I feel so much better about myself these days. I have a couple of good friends and that's great, because that wasn't so easy before. And I feel a lot calmer. I even get through my homework most days—and remember to hand it in. It feels good to know I can do that.

—Trevor, age 14

Life is filled with challenges. This is true whether or not you have ADHD. We cannot avoid all the difficulties that life throws at us, but we can make choices that change the way we experience those difficulties, even if many of them are out of our control.

What makes the difference between someone who rides the waves of challenges and someone who feels like they are underwater instead is often this: the wave rider has learned how to approach the waves with skill. The choices are to get pounded by the waves, to sit on the beach and watch others have fun, or to grab a surfboard and hop on.

This book offers you an array of different tools and practices that help you get up on your surfboard. Mindfulness helps you settle and see things clearly. Our minds are like snow globes. When you shake a snow globe, the flakes make the globe cloudy. In our minds, thoughts and emotions get stirred up and bounce into each other until we can't see. When we put the snow globe down and allow it to settle, it becomes clear. Similarly, with mindfulness practice, we let our minds settle so we can see life more clearly.

At these moments, we're able to observe our mind like a scientist, staying objective and curious, putting a little distance between us and our experiences. In other words, we're no longer lost in our racing thoughts and overwhelming emotions. That allows us to make careful decisions and to let go of our stories. We see what is best for us in the long run, rather than what simply gets us through the day.

When our minds settle, something else happens. We realize that being human means that each of us is an integral member of this band of creatures roaming the earth. We are alive and breathing, and hold a unique and vital place among other humans. We are our own special version of a human with our own particular personality, quirks, brand of humor, and way of approaching life.

On top of that, we realize something else that totally changes how we live. We realize that we're not alone. Each of us has our own challenges. Even when we feel bad about ourselves—*especially* when we feel bad about ourselves—we see that we're not alone in our struggles.

If you've gotten this far into this book, chances are your version of being human involves ADHD. What makes you *you* includes your challenges. All of you

ALL OF YOU IS PRECIOUS & DESERVES TO BE CARED FOR

together is precious and needs care. That is your key to unlocking the door to self-compassion. And that door—self-compassion—can lead you down a road to developing healthy ways to meet your challenges. It allows you to respond to the fundamental self-compassion question in any moment: what is it that I need?

When responding to this question, recognize the difference between *wants* and *needs*. Wants are from the neck up, emerging from our thinking minds. We can want a car, want a boyfriend or girlfriend, or want a new iPhone. What we want isn't always what we *need*, though.

Needs are fundamentally things that must happen so we feel complete in a sustainable way—for example, our need to be seen for who we are, our need to be listened to, our need to be loved, and our need to belong and feel connected to a group. Needs include taking care of yourself and making skilled decisions that keep you safe, productive, and on a path toward a healthy future. Be honest with yourself when asking what it is that you truly need. No one else needs to know but you.

In this book, we've provided both mindfulness and self-compassion practices so you can give yourself precisely what you need. Mindfulness and compassion—including, of course, self-compassion—are like two wings on a bird. Balance and flight require both wings, knowing exactly what's going on while building a perspective of kindness for ourselves.

If we spend time working only on awareness, we wouldn't necessarily move ahead. Awareness alone can sometimes feel too analytical. Self-compassion supports our motivation to make changes, letting go of judgment and perfectionism. Of course, compassion alone isn't enough either. We need mindful awareness to see where our struggles lie so that we can build resolve and do something about them.

In addition to practices that will help you stay mindful and self-compassionate, we've provided practical ADHD tools. To thrive, you want to know how to overcome your own ADHD, at home, in school, and in your social life and health. Use these tools—along with mindfulness and self-compassion practices—to take control of your ADHD, and start moving forward.

To review, here are just a few of those steps:

- Establish a regular mindfulness practice.

- Recognize when your inner critic shows up and decide how much you'd like to listen.

- Look out for when ADHD is making life hard. Without judging yourself for your challenges, aim to manage your ADHD fully. And then, reach out for supports and create new plans for yourself.

And as you engage with new routines to help your brain manager do its job, don't forget:

- Celebrate your successes. Remember to give yourself credit when you've accomplished even a small step toward your goal.

- Remember, there is no certain way you or your ADHD plan "should" be. We are all unique. Figure out solutions that fit your own lifestyle and strengths.

- Stay patient with yourself. Reestablishing lifetime habits takes time.

- Value your strengths. They may not be immediately apparent to you, but we all have them! You may have certain challenges, but you also have gifts and talents.

Know that you're not alone, and treat yourself with care, and you will take charge of your life and steer yourself where you want to go. For all that is uncertain, one thing guaranteed in life is that you'll face challenges. How will you meet them? Will you park your car on the shoulder and let life go by? Or end up swerving across the road? Combining mindfulness and self-compassion with all the practical ADHD-related suggestions offered here will keep your grip on the wheel, driving yourself toward a healthy, happy future.

Acknowledgments

There are many whose work we have leaned upon and who have influenced this book. We'd like to thank countless brilliant voices in the ADHD field, including good friends Drs. Ari Tuckman, Roberto Olivardia, and especially (this time around) Stephanie Sarkis for their wisdom and wit, and Dr. Russell Barkley for what he's taught us all. To so many mindfulness teachers, including Sharon Salzberg, Joseph Goldstein, Jack Kornfield, DaeJa Napier, Tara Brach, Jon Kabat-Zinn, and our various communities that have supported us on our paths over the years. We would like to also acknowledge Drs. Kristin Neff and Chris Germer, pioneers in the field of self-compassion, and creators of the Mindful Self-Compassion program. Many of the practices in this book are inspired by their work. Other practices are adapted from Making Friends with Yourself, the teen adaptation of Mindful Self-Compassion, which was created by Karen in partnership with Lorraine Hobbs. Big thanks to Alayna Fender for her social media exercise, and "Soles of the Feet," which was borrowed from Joshua Felver and Nirbhay Singh's book *Mindfulness in the Classroom.* "A Person Just Like Me" was borrowed from Trish Broderick's teen mindfulness program "Learning to BREATHE." Finally, a big thank you to Drew Kling for his expert attention and guidance.

Most of all, we would like to thank our editors, Tesilya Hanauer and Vicraj Gill, for their careful eye, tremendous patience, and expert guidance.

We thank Dale for putting up with Karen's being glued to the computer for endless hours, and Elizabeth for her vision in saving the day.

Endnotes

1   CDC. 2020. "Data and Statistics About ADHD | CDC." Atlanta, GA: Centers for Disease Control and Prevention.

2   Felver, J. C., and N. N. Singh. 2020. *Mindfulness in the Classroom.* Oakland, CA: New Harbinger Publications.

3   Adapted from Making Friends with Yourself, and inspired by the practice *Self-Compassion Break* from Mindful Self-Compassion.

4   Brown, T. 2017. *Outside the Box: Rethinking ADD/ADHD in Children and Adults: A Practical Guide.* Washington, DC: American Psychiatric Association Publishing.

5   Adapted from Making Friends with Yourself, and inspired by the practice *Appreciating Our Good Qualities* from Mindful Self-Compassion.

6   Adapted from Making Friends with Yourself, and inspired by the practice *How Would I Treat a Friend* from Mindful Self-Compassion.

7   Breines, J. G., and S. Chen. 2012. "Self-Compassion Increases Self-Improvement Motivation." *Personality and Social Psychology Bulletin,* 38(9): 1133–43.

8   Adapted from Making Friends with Yourself, and inspired by the practice *Motivating Ourselves with Compassion* from Mindful Self-Compassion.

9 Killingsworth, M. A., and D. T. Gilbert. 2010. "A Wandering Mind Is an Unhappy Mind." *Science,* 330(6006): 932.

10 Adapted from Making Friends with Yourself, and inspired by the practice *Soothing and Supportive Touch* from Mindful Self-Compassion.

11 Porges, S. W. 2011. *The Polyvagal Theory: Neurophysiological Foundations of Emotions, Attachment, Communication, and Self-Regulation* (*Norton Series on Interpersonal Neurobiology*). New York: W.W. Norton & Company.

12 Shaw, P., et al. 2014. "Emotional Dysregulation and Attention-Deficit/Hyperactivity Disorder." *The American Journal of Psychiatry* 171(3): 276–93.

13 Creswell, J. D., B. M. Way, N. I. Eisenberg, and M. D. Lieberman. 2007. "Neural Correlates of Dispositional Mindfulness During Affect Labeling." *Psychosomatic medicine,* 69(6), 560-65.

14 Inspired by an exercise from the unpublished curriculum Making Friends with Yourself.

15 Rosenberg, M. B. 2003. *Nonviolent Communication: A Language of Life.* 2nd ed. Encinitas, CA: PuddleDancer.

16 This exercise is a modified version of a practice created by Alayna Fender for Embracing Your Life, an unpublished self-compassion curriculum for young adults.

17 Twenge, J. M., and W. K. Campbell. 2018. "Associations Between Screen Time and Lower Psychological Well-Being Among Children and Adolescents: Evidence from a Population-Based Study." *Preventive Medicine Reports* 12: 271–83.

18 Adapted from P.C. Broderick and J. L. Frank. 2014. "Learning to BREATHE: An Intervention to Foster Mindfulness in Adolescence." *New Directions for Youth Development* 142: 31–44.

19 Barkley, R. A. 2006. *Attention–Deficit Hyperactivity Disorder: A Handbook for Diagnosis and Treatment.* 3rd ed. New York: The Guilford Press.

20 Inspired by a practice from the unpublished curriculum Making Friends with Yourself.

21 Dweck, C. S. 2016. *Mindset:* The *New Psychology of Success.* New York: Penguin Random House.

22 Spencer, T. J., et al. 2013. "Effect of Psychostimulants on Brain Structure and Function in ADHD: A Qualitative Literature Review of Magnetic Resonance Imaging-Based Neuroimaging Studies." *The Journal of Clinical Psychiatry* 74 (9): 902–17; Czerniak, S. M., et al. 2013. "Areas of the Brain Modulated by Single-Dose Methylphenidate Treatment in Youth with ADHD During Task-Based FMRI: A Systematic Review." *Harvard Review of Psychiatry* 21(3): 151–62.

23 Harstad, E. B., et al. 2014. "ADHD, Stimulant Treatment, and Growth: A Longitudinal Study." *Pediatrics* 134(4):935–44.

Mark Bertin, MD, is a developmental pediatrician in private practice in Pleasantville, NY. He is author of *How Children Thrive* and *Mindful Parenting for ADHD*, which integrate mindfulness into the rest of evidence-based pediatric care; and a contributing author for *Teaching Mindfulness Skills to Kids and Teens*. He is on faculty at New York Medical College and The Windward Institute, on advisory boards for Common Sense Media and Reach Out and Read, and on the board of directors for APSARD (the American Professional Society of ADHD and Related Disorders). His blog covering topics in child development, mindfulness, and family is available through PsychologyToday.com, Mindful.org, and elsewhere. For information about his online mindfulness classes and other resources, visit https://developmentaldoctor.com.

Karen Bluth, PhD, is on faculty in the department of psychiatry and a research fellow at Frank Porter Graham Child Development Institute at the University of North Carolina at Chapel Hill, where she is founder of the Frank Porter Graham Program on Mindfulness and Self-Compassion for Families (https://selfcompas sion.web.unc.edu). She is a certified instructor of Mindful Self-Compassion, an internationally acclaimed eight-week course created by Kristin Neff and Christopher Germer; and is a codeveloper of Self-Compassion for Educators, a self-compassion program offered through Mindful Schools.

Bluth is also cocreator of the curriculum Making Friends with Yourself: A Mindful Self-Compassion Program for Teens, the teen adaptation of Mindful Self-Compassion; and Embracing Your Life, the young adult adaptation. She is also author of *The Self-Compassion Workbook for Teens* and *The Self-Compassionate Teen*. As a mindfulness practitioner for more than forty years, a mindfulness teacher, and an educator with eighteen years of classroom teaching experience, Bluth frequently gives talks, conducts workshops, and teaches classes in self-compassion and mindfulness in educational and community settings. In addition, she trains teachers in Making Friends with Yourself internationally.

More ⏱Instant Help Books for Teens

An Imprint of New Harbinger Publications

THE EXECUTIVE FUNCTIONING WORKBOOK FOR TEENS

Help for Unprepared, Late, and Scattered Teens

978-1608826568 / US $17.95

THE STRESS REDUCTION WORKBOOK FOR TEENS, SECOND EDITION

Mindfulness Skills to Help You Deal with Stress

978-1684030187 / US $16.95

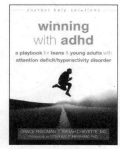

WINNING WITH ADHD

A Playbook for Teens and Young Adults with Attention Deficit/ Hyperactivity Disorder

978-1684031658 / US $16.95

STUFF THAT SUCKS

A Teen's Guide to Accepting What You Can't Change and Committing to What You Can

978-1626258655 / US $14.95

THE GROWTH MINDSET WORKBOOK FOR TEENS

Say Yes to Challenges, Deal with Difficult Emotions, and Reach Your Full Potential

978-1684035571 / US $18.95

JUST AS YOU ARE

A Teen's Guide to Self-Acceptance and Lasting Self-Esteem

978-1626255906 / US $16.95

🍃 **newharbinger**publications

1-800-748-6273 / newharbinger.com

(VISA, MC, AMEX / prices subject to change without notice)   Follow Us 📷 ⓕ 🅨 ▶ ⓟ ⓛ

Don't miss out on new books in the subjects that interest you.
Sign up for our Book Alerts at **newharbinger.com/bookalerts**